The Vietnam War and Public Policy

by
Melvin Sharp

Copyright 1991

A REAL WORLD SOCIAL STUDIES Publication
from
POLICY STUDIES ASSOCIATES

Policy Studies Associates (PSA) was established in 1976 to help develop policy analysis skills and apply these to important public issues. An operating program of the Council on International and Public Affairs, PSA is a cooperative non-profit undertaking of a small group of faculty members, teachers, and other educators concerned with improving the quality of education on public policy issues in schools, colleges, and universities.

In 1986, PSA initiated the Effective Participation in Government Program (EPG) to assist secondary schools, teachers, and students in introducing courses of study which emphasize informal participation in government and community affairs. In 1990, EPG became REAL WORLD SOCIAL STUDIES and grew to include materials for middle and lower schools as well. Real World Social Studies organizes teacher workshops, provides consultative assistance to schools, and publishes instructional material for teachers and students. For further information on program content, write: Real World Social Studies, P.O. Box 632, Fayetteville, New York 13066. Ordering inquiries should be directed to Policy Studies Associates, Box 337, Croton-on-Hudson, New York 10520.

ACKNOWLEDGEMENTS

The Vietnam War and Public Policy evolved from a course project I did in 1990 at the State University of New York at New Paltz. The course, *America in Vietnam*, is taught by Dr. David Krikun. Dr. Krikun challenges his students to read the most current and authoritative books on the war. In addition, he assigns a course project that is to have real applications in the classroom. I have always wanted to teach a high school or undergraduate course on the war. Dr. Krikun encouraged me to find a way to use the war in my Participation in Government curriculum. Therein was born the idea to teach about the Vietnam War through a public policy perspective.

Dr. Krikun has provided invaluable assistance in reviewing the book and providing honest and constructive criticism. I am deeply indebted to him for his support of this project, his expertise, and his friendship. His only goal was the unselfish one of making this the best book I could write on the subject.

Dr. William Coplin, Professor of Public Affairs and Director of the Public Affairs Program of the Maxwell School at Syracuse University, has been my liaison at Real World Social Studies. I am grateful to him for his permission to pirate his model of public policy analysis and to Real World Social Studies for their publication of books that have true classroom value.

I am also grateful to the outstanding editor of Real World Social Studies, Maryrose Eannace. She has provided just the right amount of criticism and support for my writing. Editing is more than dotting i's and crossing t's; its something akin to being a football coach, one part objective critic and one part subjective fan.

In addition, I thank Christopher LaVallee and Maya Saxen for their invaluable manuscript preparation.

Lastly, I'd like to thank my wife Cyndi and my daughter Sonya for their patience and support. Their encouragement has led me in a few short years from a job filled with frustration to fulfillment of a lifetime ambition.

Melvin (Jim) Sharp
June 1991

ABOUT THE AUTHOR

Mel Sharp teaches Participation in Government, U.S. History, and Economics at Goshen High School in Goshen, New York. After earning his Bachelors in Economics from Cook College of Rutgers University, he spent ten years in industry and two years restoring a two hundred year old house before returning to school to earn his Certification and his Master's Degree (SUNY at New Paltz). He finds teaching to be the most fulfilling of careers.

Mr. Sharp's serious interest in the Vietnam War began when he drew #256 in the draft lottery during his senior year in high school. The year was 1972 and our involvement in the Vietnam War was nearly at an end. Mr. Sharp's interest did not end, however, and a new dimension was added as he observed the treatment returning Vietnam Vets received. His personal interest has fueled an academic study that has resulted in a highly successful and popular course on public policy and the War. This book is a result of his desire to share his vast knowledge and unique perspective of the U.S. involvement in the Vietnam War.

Mr. Sharp lives in Port Jervis, New York with his wife, Cyndi and his daughter, Sonya. He is already at work on his next book.

Dedication

This book is dedicated to my father and to all veterans of armed combat everywhere. May we never take their sacrifices lightly nor send them into battle without just cause.

Note to Students

In each chapter you will find a series of checkpoint questions. You should review them carefully to test your knowledge. Your instructor may also wish to assign the checkpoint questions as written assignments or as topics for classroom discussion.

Table of Contents

TIMETABLE OF EVENTS

1954
French surrender at Dienbienphu
Geneva Agreements

1955
Diem "elected" President of SVN
SVN refuses reunification vote

1956
Communists pursue political struggle in the South
American advisers, sent by Eisenhower, train SVN army

1959
PAVN begins supplying arms to cadres in the South

1960
Armed struggle begins in the South

1962
JFK increases advisers to 11,000

1963
Thich Quang Duc's self-immolation
Diem killed, followed by Minh, Don, and Khiem

1964
Khahn follows Minh and Don
Gulf of Tonkin Resolution

1965
Ky and Thieu follow Khahn
Rolling Thunder and U.S. ground troops

1967
Demonstrations in U.S. and Vietnam against the War
U.S. claims end of war in sight

1968
Tet Offensive
U.S. public opinion -- more than 50% oppose war
Bombing of North suspended
Negotiations begin

1969
Nixon announces Vietnamization
U.S. bombs communist bases in Cambodia

1970
U.S. ground troops used in Cambodia
Massive protests in the U.S.

1972
Kissinger announces peace is at hand
PAVN launches massive invasion on two fronts
U.S. resumes bombing the North

1973
Last U.S. troops withdrawn
War Powers Act passed

1975
Vietnam reunified
PAVN units take Saigon
Massive exodus of pro-U.S. Vietnamese

GLOSSARY OF ACRONYMS

ARVN - Army of the Republic of Vietnam, the South Vietnamese army.

CIA - Central Intelligence Agency of the U.S., the arm of the executive branch charged with gathering information.

DRV - also NVN, (North Vietnam), the Democratic Republic of Vietnam.

KIA - killed in action.

MIA - missing in action.

NLF - National Liberation Front, nationalist communist party in the South.

PAVN -also NVA, (North Vietnamese Army), the regular army of the DRV.

PLAF -People's Liberation Armed Forces, the army of the NLF.

POW - prisoner of war.

PTSD -post-traumatic stress disorder, a combat induced mental illness suffered by some Vietnam vets.

ROTC - Reserve Officers Training Corps (United States).

RVN - also SVN, (South Vietnam), the Republic of Vietnam.

SDS - Students for a Democratic Society (United States).

SEATO - Southeast Asia Treaty Organization.

VC - Vietcong, a derogatory term used by Americans for the NLF and the PLAF.

Chapter One

The Vietnam War and Public Policy

VIETNAM WAR STATISTICS

Deaths (combat)
American and Vietnamese   1,979,135+

Missing in Action
American   2,500

U.S. Soldier
Average age   19 years old

Defoliants and Herbicides Used
in gallons   18,000,000

Bombs dropped by U.S.
in tons   17,000,000

Financial cost of the war
estimated $1,000,000,000

Introduction

As dramatic as the preceding costs of the Vietnam War are, they do not tell the whole story nor the total cost of that war. In the aftermath of the Persian Gulf War (1991), we are again asking questions about the war in Vietnam and weighing its costs to our nation. Teachers and students, veterans and intellectuals, politicians and citizens, all have renewed interest in the Vietnam War, the longest, and in some ways, the most divisive war in American history.

Interest in the war has been expressed in the continuing volume of material, both in print and film, devoted to the war. The jingoism of *Rambo* and the stark realism of *Platoon* or *Born on the Fourth of July*, show an America haunted by the images of Vietnam.

People in their teens and twenties are looking for the source of society's pervasive disillusionment with politics, anxiety over military service, and questions of values and political assumptions. If you are of this searching generation, you may have asked your parents, "What did you do in the war?" Within that question lie many others: *Were you a protestor or a soldier? Did people play roles other than those portrayed in the movies? How did you feel about the war?* Examination of the issues surrounding the war can give two generations some common basis for discussion and understanding.

Two of the most long-lasting effects of the war have been a distrust of government and general apathy toward working for positive change. As these attitudes became more ingrained, it is no wonder that the "we generation" of the sixties became the "me generation" that followed. The Vietnam War has left us a legacy of pervasive disillusionment with politics, anxiety over military service, and questions of values and political assumptions. As today's students question and search for a better, more vital mode, they look to the experiences of the sixties and of the Vietnam War, and they examine the culture shaped by the war's lessons.

Vietnam

People have asked, "Why did we get involved in a country *half a world away*?" But Vietnam is, in many ways, much more than geographically distant from the U.S. It is a small country, not much larger than the state of Florida. It is a traditional society shaped by an Eastern religion, Buddhism, and a Chinese philosophical system, Confucianism. It is affected by weather conditions unknown in the continental U.S. such as monsoons, and tropical heat. Its terrain varies from dense forest to rugged mountains to river deltas. It is an agriculturally-based society dependent on rice. It is strategically situated in Southeast Asia with a long (1000 mile) coastline and fine natural harbors. It is an ancient culture with a rich legacy of art, poetry, prose, and myth.

It is also a country that has assimilated much from cultures of invaders without losing its own identity. This identity has been preserved through Vietnamese nationalism. From 1954 to 1973, Vietnamese nationalism clashed with American foreign policy interests and the costs to both countries were enormous.

3

Public Policy Analysis

The development of U.S. policy on the Vietnam War is a study in public policy analysis. To fully understand the how and why of our involvement in the Vietnam War, we must first understand the basics of public policy -- how it is formed, altered, and put into effect.

What is a public policy ?

We might want to think of public policy as rules, laws, or guidelines.
Public policy is a government action designed to have an impact on a social condition.

Public policy is not just something that Congress enacts and the President signs. Public policy exists at all levels of society including the classroom level. Rules on smoking and attendance are examples of classroom public policy.

When does public policy become an issue ?

For a public policy to become a public policy **issue**, three conditions must be present:

1. There must be a public policy involved. Ask yourself, is there an existing or proposed government action involved?

2. The policy must be designed to have an impact on a social condition. Examples of social conditions include homelessness, drug and alcohol abuse, the trade deficit. Examples of social conditions in the school may include racial conflicts or the rights of smokers vs. non-smokers.

4

3. There must be disagreement between *players* over the policy *or* the social conditions. A **player** is an individual or organization that works to shape public policy. For example, people who smoke in public places may see nothing wrong with the social condition that others find objectionable. Or they may disagree over the policy that forbids smoking in certain locations. Players on the smoking issue may include smokers, non-smokers, tobacco companies, medical organizations and government.

In review, to decide if something is a public policy issue, you must answer yes to each of the following questions.

1. Is a public policy involved?

2. Is that policy designed to have an impact on a social condition?

3. Is there disagreement among players over the policy or the social conditions?

Identifying Goals of Players

What motivates players to feel and act in certain ways on public policy issues? Our understanding of players' goals aids us in public policy analysis. Players' goals may be seen in their writings, speeches, and actions and may be inferred from analysis of their circumstances, position, or interests.

Knowing the goals of players helps us to better appreciate their point of view and can often lead conflicting players to explore compromises. This is the essence of the political process. Players seek to gain wider support for their goals by publicly explaining those goals.

Goals that will benefit society as a whole are known as *public interests*. Examples of public interests include public safety, national defense, social justice, and due process of law.

Other goals may be more private in nature. *Private interest goals* benefit the player directly and exclusively. These goals are usually economic in nature and may not be spoken of in public discussions on a public policy issue. The reason for keeping these goals quiet is obvious; since the benefit is received exclusively and directly by the player, the player will gain little, if any, public support by making his or her true motives known.

It is vitally important in looking at public policy issues that we examine both the private and the public interests of players. What is left unspoken may be just as important as those things that are publicly professed.

Checkpoint

Which of these are public policy issues? For those that are not public policy issues, state why they are not.

1. A hurricane hits a small town in Florida and many buildings are destroyed.

2. Your student government sponsors a dialogue between administrators and students who have differing viewpoints on the lateness policy.

3. The National Rifle Association mounts a campaign to defeat a bill designed to limit handgun sales.

4. Skateboarding is banned in your town. Skateboard enthusiasts ask that a park be built for them.

5. State aid to your town increases and property taxes fall.

continued...

Checkpoint (continued)

In each scenario below, identify a player on each side of the issue and identify a public and a private interest for each player.

1. The street on which Bill lives is full of potholes. He petitions the town board for repairs. People on the other side of town oppose these repairs due to anticipated tax increases.

2. A rock group, known for its explicit lyrics, plans to play at a local high school. Parents organize opposition.

3. The Secretary of Defense asks Congress for a 20% increase in the defense budget.

4. The governor vetoes legislation designed to create a death penalty for drug kingpins.

Chapter Two

The Roots of the Conflict

In *The Vietnam War and Public Policy*, we will explore how American foreign policy toward Vietnam developed over the years and how that foreign policy was a reflection of three things: internal developments in Vietnam, internal developments in the U.S., and the foreign policy of the U.S.

As you read the chapter narrative and the readings that are included, try to identify the forces that shaped public policy on the Vietnam War. Particularly, try to identify key players, their goals, and their public and private interests.

A Brief History of Vietnam

When the U.S. decided to commit ground troops to the war in Vietnam in 1965, the North Vietnamese resigned themselves to a new war and a new foe. The history of Vietnam is full of such instances in which a foreign power tried to impose a new government or order. In each case, the people of Vietnam were able to remove the foreign presence. The Chinese ruled Vietnam for more than a thousand years and were expelled in 938 A.D. Over the following four centuries, the Vietnamese successfully defended their independence against the Mongols and, once again, the Chinese.

In the mid-nineteenth century, France began expansionist invasions of Vietnam that, by 1883, resulted in French colonization of Vietnam. French control lasted until 1954, interrupted only by a brief period of Japanese control in World War II. In 1954, Vietnam was partitioned, or divided, in two, with the Vietminh-led North being supported by the Soviets and the South being supported by the U.S. The U.S. presence would last for nearly twenty years, but once again the Vietnamese people were able to re-establish control over their own country.

This legacy of war in defense of nationhood has led the Vietnamese people to three important beliefs that help explain the failure of U.S. foreign policy in Vietnam in the period from 1945 to 1975.

The first of these beliefs is called the *myth of national indomitability*, a belief that the Vietnamese people are not easily defeated or discouraged. Nationalism and history point to the fact that the Vietnamese have been able to repeatedly defeat foes who possessed greater technology and firepower. As a result, the Vietnamese feel they cannot be beaten.

The second belief that bolsters this feeling of indomitability is the Vietnamese belief that the will of the people, when properly ignited, can defeat any opponent regardless of the opponent's abilities. This theory is based on winning the hearts and minds of the people to the cause of nationalism. As we shall see, this battle was fought through education, propaganda, terrorism, and assassination, as well as on the battlefield.

The final belief can only be understood by understanding the Vietnamese concept of time. A nation that measures its history in millenniums (thousands of years) has a much different perspective from that of a "young" nation like the United States. Any occupying force in Vietnam is seen as expeditionary, that is, there temporarily. Some historians argue that it was this belief in the temporary nature of U.S. forces in Vietnam that doomed the U.S. to failure in its military attempts. The North (North Vietnam), saw the U.S. commitment as temporary and resigned itself to a war of attrition (gradually wearing down the resolve of the U.S.). Together, the forces of the myth of national indomitability, the belief in the will of the masses, and the keen sense of national identity through the ages, have forged a country unique in history.

This keen sense of national identity has remained intact through Vietnamese history. Over the centuries, the Vietnamese people have forged this strong sense of nationalism through the factors described above and through an assimilation of Chinese culture. This assimilation occurred during the thousand year Chinese occupation of Vietnam. Vietnam fell victim to a Chinese version of Manifest Destiny in the second century B.C. The Chinese felt it was their duty to bring to Vietnam their advanced systems of government, science, philosophy, literature, art and language. The most enduring of these gifts was the philosophy known as Confucianism. The Vietnamese adopted the Confucian beliefs that emphasized a well-educated power elite with a strong sense of history.

11

This knowledge of history helped maintain Vietnamese nationalism through a millennium of Chinese rule.

Confucianism had other effects on Vietnam that helped shape Vietnamese nationalism. This philosophical system brought to Vietnam a strong civil service system based on merit and a reverence for teachers and education. The power of the monarch was limited by a broad set of ethical principles and an emperor who disregarded these principles risked losing his throne. Confucianism also placed emphasis on the family as the building block of the nation. Public service was looked on as a worthy and important occupation. All of these factors helped build a central core of Vietnamese nationalists with a deep sense of history and a cultural identity that absorbed China's legacy but remained essentially Vietnamese.

We have said that Vietnam is a unique nation. The U.S. is also a unique nation forged by influences quite different from Confucianism. We have developed a strong sense of national identity through a marvelous democratic heritage. One of the key questions we will deal with is how these two cultures came to be on a collision course in the mid-twentieth century. The story is one of a clash of cultures; a meeting of the values and belief systems of the East and the West. It is also a study in the formation and execution of public policy on both an international and domestic scale. It is a study in politics and it is full of lessons for today's and future leaders.

Vietnam Between the World Wars

The French ruthlessly exploited Vietnam during their occupation. Peasants were reduced to near starvation and the country was robbed of its minerals and agricultural products. Vietnamese were denied any high office and anyone who spoke out against the French risked imprisonment or a worse fate. The French disrupted a traditional society based on Confucianism and Buddhism and thrust Vietnam into the international economy by exporting its rice and rubber. All profits went to French companies such as Michelin. This economic and political oppression made for a country ripe for revolution.

The Treaty of Versailles (1919), which established the League of Nations, brought hope to nationalist forces worldwide with its pledges of self-determination of nations, that is, the right of a people to decide on their own form of government. Western nations like the U.S., Great Britain, and France paid lip service to this concept while continuing to maintain colonies or overseas territories. The Soviet leader, Lenin, called for an end to colonialism and championed the overthrow of colonialist powers and the emergence of new, independent countries.

A young Vietnamese by the name of Nguyen Tat Thanh, working in Paris in 1920, was attracted to Lenin's condemnation of colonialism and became a communist. He helped found the French Communist Party and moved on to study in Moscow in 1924. By 1930 he had found his way to southern China where he founded the Indochinese Communist Party. He returned to Vietnam in 1941 to try to realize his dream of Vietnamese independence. Upon his return to Vietnam he assumed the name Ho Chi Minh. In time, he would be known as the George Washington of Vietnam.

Ho realized that capitalism and colonialism were tied

together. He felt that Marxism and its renunciation of imperialism and colonialism provided an effective means of achieving nationhood. He felt betrayed by the broken promises that the West had made in the Versailles Treaty. Ho worked for thirty years to channel Vietnamese nationalism in the direction of communism. He never saw his dream of independence realized.

The First Indochina War - 1941 to 1954

In August of 1941, Franklin Roosevelt and Winston Churchill met aboard a ship in the stormy waters off Newfoundland. Together they developed a plan for the prosecution of WWII and their vision of the post-war world. This plan was called the Atlantic Charter. Among its provisions was a call, once again, for self-determination of nations. This proposal was warmly received by the revolutionary forces of Vietnam. In 1941, the Vietminh (League for the Independence of Vietnam) was formed to try to lead Vietnam away from French colonialism and toward independence.

Ho Chi Minh emerged as its leader and his followers approached American intelligence officers operating in Vietnam and volunteered to help find downed American pilots and provide information on Japanese troop movements. The U.S. eagerly accepted this aid and provided Ho with radios and small arms. Buoyed by this alliance and the promises of the Atlantic Charter, the Vietminh hoped for an end to French colonial rule after the end of the war. With the defeat of the Japanese in 1945, the Vietminh pressed forward and took control of much of northern Vietnam and established a capital at Hanoi. The August

14

Revolution brought to power various groups throughout Vietnam that were allied with the Vietminh. The French puppet Bao Dai was chased from the throne and Ho Chi Minh named himself president. The Vietminh then published the Vietnamese Declaration of Independence. As you read this document, try to answer the following questions:

Checkpoint

1. How is this document similar, in form and content, to the Declaration of Independence of the American colonies?

2. Why did Ho Chi Minh use this form and cite the revolutions in America and France in the eighteenth century?

3. What is the importance of the mention of the conferences at Teheran and San Francisco?

The Vietnamese Declaration of Independence
1945

All men are created equal; they are endowed by their Creator with certain unalienable Rights; among these are Life, Liberty, and the pursuit of Happiness.

This immortal statement was made in the Declaration of Independence of the United States of America in 1776. In a broader sense, this means: All the peoples on the earth are equal from birth, all peoples have a right to live, to be happy and free.

The Declaration of the French Revolution made in 1791 on the Rights of Man and the Citizen also states: "All men are born free and with equal rights, and must always remain free and have equal rights."

Those are undeniable truths.

Nevertheless, for more than eighty years, French imperialists, abusing the standard of Liberty, Equality, and Fraternity, have violated our Fatherland and oppressed our fellow citizens. They have acted contrary to the ideals of humanity and justice.

In the field of politics, they have deprived our people of every democratic liberty.

They have enforced inhuman laws; they have set up three distinct political regimes in the North, the Center, and the South of Viet-Nam in order to wreck our national unity and prevent our people from being united.

They have built more prisons than schools. They have mercilessly slain our patriots; they have drowned our uprisings in rivers of blood.

They have fettered public opinion; they have practiced obscurantism against our people.

To weaken our race they have forced us to use opium and alcohol.

In the field of economics, they have fleeced us to the backbone, impoverished our people and devastated our land.

They have robbed us of our rice fields, our mines, our forests, and our raw materials. They have monopolized the issuing of bank notes and the export trade.

They have invented numerous unjustifiable taxes and reduced our people, especially our peasantry, to a state of extreme poverty.

They have hampered the prospering of our national bourgeoisie; they have mercilessly exploited our workers.

In the autumn of 1940, when the Japanese fascists violated Indochina's territory to establish new bases in their fight against the Allies, the French imperialists went down on their bended knees and handed over our country to them.

Thus, from that date, our people were subjected to the

double yoke of the French and the Japanese. Their sufferings and miseries increased. The result was that, from the end of last year to the beginning of this year, from Quang Tri Province to the North of Viet-Nam, more than two million of our fellow citizens died from starvation. On March 9 [1945], the French troops were disarmed by the Japanese. The French colonialists either fled or surrendered, showing that not only were they incapable of "protecting" us, but that, in the span of five years, they had twice sold our country to the Japanese.

On several occasions before March 9, the Viet Minh League urged the French to ally themselves with it against the Japanese. Instead of agreeing to this proposal, the French colonialists so intensified their terrorist activities against the Viet Minh members that before fleeing they massacred a great number of our political prisoners detained at Yen Bay and Cao Bang.

Notwithstanding all this, our fellow citizens have always manifested toward the French a tolerant and humane attitude. Even after the Japanese *Putsch* of March, 1945, the Viet Minh League helped many Frenchmen to cross the frontier, rescued some of them from Japanese jails, and protected French lives and property.

From the autumn of 1940, our country had in fact ceased to be a French Colony and had become a Japanese possession.

After the Japanese had surrendered to the Allies, our whole people rose to regain our national sovereignty and to found the Democratic Republic of Viet-Nam.

The truth is that we have wrested our independence from the Japanese and not from the French.

The French have fled, the Japanese have capitulated, Emperor Bao Dai has abdicated. Our people have broken the chains which for nearly a century have fettered them and have won independence for the Fatherland. Our people at the same time have overthrown the monarchic regime that has reigned supreme for dozens of centuries. In its place has been established the present Democratic Republic.

For these reasons, we, members of the Provisional Government, representing the whole Vietnamese people, declare that from now on we break off all relations of a colonial character with France; we repeal all the international

17

obligation that France has so far subscribed to on behalf of Viet-Nam, and we abolish all the special rights the French have unlawfully acquired in our Fatherland.

The whole Vietnamese people, animated by a common purpose, are determined to fight to the bitter end against any attempt by the French colonialists to reconquer their country.

We are convinced that the Allied nations, which at Teheran and San Francisco have acknowledged the principles of self-determination and equality of nations, will not refuse to acknowledge the independence of Viet-Nam.

A people who have courageously opposed French domination for more than eighty years, a people who have fought side by side with the Allies against the fascists during these last years, such a people must be free and independent.

For these reasons, we, members of the Provisional Government of the Democratic Republic of Viet-Nam, solemnly declare to the world that Viet-Nam has the right to be a free and independent country - and in fact it is so already. The entire Vietnamese people are determined to mobilize all their physical and mental strength, to sacrifice their lives and property in order to safeguard their independence and liberty.

Policy of Containment

The French were unwilling to give up their prized colony and fought back against the communist forces to regain control of Vietnam. The U.S. again dismissed the ideal of self-determination of nations and supported the continued French colonial government. The reasons for this were many but can be summed up in the U.S. *policy of containment*.

After WWII, the Soviet Union maintained the countries of Eastern Europe as buffer states and tried to expand its sphere of influence in the Mediterranean. In 1949, China became a communist country and communists began

18

winning small but important election victories in France. These, and other factors, created a perception in the U.S. of the need for a foreign policy designed to "contain" the spread of communism. This policy included economic and, if necessary, military aid to countries threatened by the spread of communism. In the same year that China became communist, France attempted to placate the nationalist forces in Vietnam by declaring Vietnam to be a "free state within the French Union."

This did not satisfy the Vietminh's quest for an independent nation. Negotiations with the Vietminh broke down and from 1946 to 1954 the Vietminh waged a war of independence against the French. The U.S. initially tried to stay out of the situation in Indochina because the U.S. was preoccupied with communist attempts at expansionism in Eastern Europe, Turkey, and Greece. However, despite the promises of the Atlantic Charter, the U.S. government backed the continued French presence in Vietnam for two reasons. First, the French government was under increasing pressure from the rising communist party in France. The loss of prestige that would have accompanied the loss of French colonies in Indochina might have been politically embarrassing enough to topple the pro-U.S. ruling party and catapult the communists to power in France. Secondly, the U.S. began to see the struggle against the Vietminh as just another front in the war to contain communism.

U.S. involvement in Korea convinced American policy makers to begin direct military aid to the French in Vietnam in 1950. It would be twenty-three years before the U.S. would stop the war effort in Vietnam.

Another Historical Analogy

Before his death, President Franklin D. Roosevelt, warned his advisers of the growing intransigence (refusal to compromise) of the Soviet Union. He had been willing to side with the Soviets in defense against common enemies in WWII. But, he feared and distrusted the Soviets and made this plain to his vice-president, Harry Truman. Truman, a straight-speaking Mid-Westerner, assumed the Office of President after FDR's death and had to deal with a new kind of war: the Cold War. Truman saw Soviet expansionism in many places around the world from Europe to Korea to Vietnam. In the speech that follows, Truman makes several important points about the nature, goals, and tactics of communism. These observations formed the basis for U.S. foreign policy in dealing with the Soviet Union and China in the 1950's. Pay particular attention, in the opening paragraph, to the use of historical analogy, that is, the idea that certain similarities between different countries' histories imply further similarities. In talking about WWII, Truman is referring to the Munich Analogy. In 1938, Hitler met with representatives of Great Britain and France in Munich. Hitler stated Germany's claim to the Sudetenland, a portion of Czechoslovakia. France and Great Britain agreed to the demand in return for a promise from Hitler of no further territorial expansion. Hitler soon "forgot" this promise and set in motion his plan to conquer all of Europe. This attempt at appeasement actually encouraged Hitler's expansionism. Truman, and many others since, have cited the Munich Analogy as proof that you cannot placate a bully with concessions but must meet him firmly, with force if necessary. This is a lesson most recently applied in the Persian Gulf War. As you read Truman's speech on the Munich Analogy and the international communist conspiracy, try to answer the following questions:

Checkpoint

1. After this speech, analysts begin to call communism "monolithic." What do you think that term means with respect to the USSR and China in the 1950's? Is communism monolithic today?

2. Truman says "We believe that Korea belongs to the Koreans, we believe that India belongs to the Indians, we believe that all the nations of Asia should be free to work out their affairs in their own way." Was this philosophy consistently applied in U.S. relations with Asia? What was different about the situation in Vietnam?

3. Truman recognizes China as an important constraint on U.S. policy in the Far East. Why does he fear widening the war to include the Chinese who he sees as one of the aggressors?

Harry S. Truman, Radio Report to the American People on Korea and on U.S. Policy in the Far East, April 11, 1951.

...The communists in the Kremlin are engaged in a Monstrous conspiracy to stamp out freedom all over the world. If they were to succeed, the United States would be numbered among their principal victims. It must be clear to everyone that the United States cannot -- and will not -- sit idly by and await foreign conquest. The only question is: What is the best time to meet the threat and how is the best way to meet it?

The best time to meet the threat is in the beginning. It is easier to put out a fire in the beginning when it is small than

22

after it has become a roaring blaze. And the best way to meet the threat of aggression is for the peace-loving nations to act together. If they don't act together, they are likely to be picked off, one by one.

If they had followed the right policies in the 1930's -- if the free countries had acted together to crush the aggression of the dictators, and if they had acted in the beginning when the aggression was small -- there probably would have been no World War II.

If history has taught us anything, it is that aggression anywhere in the world is a threat to the peace everywhere in the world. When that aggression is supported by the cruel and selfish rulers of a powerful nation who are bent on conquest, it becomes a clear and present danger to the security and independence of every free nation.

This is a lesson that most people in this country have learned thoroughly. This is the basic reason why we joined in creating the United Nations. And, since the end of World War II, we have been putting that lesson into practice -- we have been working with other free nations to check the aggressive designs of the Soviet Nation before they can result in a third world war.

That is what we did in Greece, when the nation was threatened by the aggression of international communism.

The attack against Greece could have led to general war. But this country came to the aid of Greece. The United Nations supported the Greek resistance. With our help, the determination and efforts of the Greek people defeated the attack on the spot.

Another big Communist threat to peace was the Berlin blockade. That too could have led to war. But again it was settled because free men would not back down in an emergency.

The aggression against Korea is the boldest and most dangerous move the Communists have yet made.

The attack on Korea was part of a greater plan for conquering all of Asia.

I would like to read to you from a secret intelligence report which came to us after the attack on Korea. It is a report of a speech a Communist army officer in North Korea gave to a group of spies and saboteurs last May, one month before South Korea was invaded. The report shows in great detail how this invasion was part of a carefully prepared plot. Here, in part, is what the Communist officer, who had been trained in Moscow, told his men: "Our forces," he said, "are scheduled to attack South Korean forces about the middle of June. The coming attack on South Korea marks the first step toward the liberation of Asia."

Notice that he used the word "liberation." This is Communist doubletalk meaning "conquest."

I have another secret intelligence report here. This one tells what another Communist officer in the Far East told his men several months before the invasion of Korea. Here is what he said: "In order to successfully undertake the long-awaited world revolution, we must first unify Asia....Java, Indochina, Malaya, India, Tibet, Thailand, Philippines, and Japan are our ultimate targets....The United States is the only obstacle on our road for the liberation of all the countries in southeast Asia. In other words, we must unify the people of Asia and crush the United States." Again, "liberation" in "commie" language means conquest.

That is what the Communist leaders are telling their people, and that is what they have been trying to do.

They want to control all Asia from the Kremlin.

This plan of conquest is in flat contradiction to what we believe. We believe that Korea belongs to the Koreans, we believe that India belongs to the Indians, we believe that all the nations of Asia should be free to work out their affairs in their own way. This is the basis of peace in the Far East, and it is the basis of peace everywhere else.

The whole Communist imperialism is back of the attack on peace in the Far East. It was the Soviet Union that trained and equipped the North Koreans for aggression. The Chinese Communists massed 44 well-trained and well-equipped divisions on the Korean frontier. They were the troops they threw into battle when the North Korean Communists were beaten.

The question we have had to face is whether the Communist plan of conquest can be stopped without a general war. Our government and other countries associated with us in the

24

United Nations believe that the best chance of stopping it without a general war is to meet the attack in Korea and defeat it there.

That is what we have been doing. It is a difficult and bitter task.

But so far it has been successful.

So far, we have prevented world war III.

So far, by fighting a limited war in Korea, we have prevented aggression from succeeding, and bringing on a general war. And the ability of the whole free world to resist Communist aggression has been greatly improved.

We have taught the enemy a lesson. He has found that aggression is not cheap or easy. Moreover, men all over the world who want to remain free have been given new courage and new hope. They know now that the champions of freedom can stand up and fight, and that they will stand up and fight.

Our resolute stand in Korea is helping the forces of freedom now fighting in Indochina and other countries in that part of the world. It has already slowed down the timetable of conquest.

In Korea itself there are signs that the enemy is building up ground forces for a new mass offensive. We also know that there have been large increases in the enemy's available air forces.

If a new attack comes, I feel confident that it will be turned back. The United Nations fighting forces are tough and able and well equipped. They are fighting for a just cause. They are proving to all the world that the principle of collective security will work. We are proud of these forces for the magnificent job they have done against heavy odds. We pray that their efforts succeed, for upon their success may hinge the peace of the world.

The Communist side must now choose its course of action. The Communist rulers may press the attack against us. They may take further action that may spread the conflict. They have that choice, and with it the awful responsibility for what may follow. The Communists also have the choice of a peaceful settlement which could lead to a general relaxation of the tensions in the Far East. The decision is theirs, because the forces of the United Nations will strive to limit the conflict if

25

possible.

We do not want to see the conflict in Korea extended. We are trying to prevent a world war -- not start one. And the best way to do that is to make it plain that we and the other free countries will continue to resist the attack.

But you may ask why can't we take other steps to punish the aggressor. Why don't we bomb Manchuria and China itself? Why don't we assist the Chinese Nationalist troops to land on the mainland of China?

If we were to do these things we would be running a very grave risk of starting a general war. If that were to happen, we would have brought about the exact situation we are trying to prevent.

If we were to do these things, we would be entangled in a vast conflict on the continent of Asia and our task would become immeasurably more difficult all over the world.

What would suit the ambitions of the Kremlin better than for our military forces to be committed to a full-scale war with Red China?...

Fateful Decisions

Historians sometimes look at the development of policy as a series of important or fateful decisions, that is decisions that will have long-term consequences for a nation. As we go through the history of U.S. involvement in Vietnam, look for these fateful decisions and also try to determine the extent of public debate about these decisions. In this chapter, we have discussed the first of these fateful decisions, the decision to support the continued French presence in Vietnam and to ignore the promises of self-determination of nations made in the Treaty of Versailles and the Atlantic Charter. In examining these decisions, we must ask: Who were the players involved? Was the decision open to public debate and if not, why not?

The decision to support the French, like many of the fateful decisions to follow on Vietnam, was confined to a small group of influential insiders including Truman, George Marshall (Secretary of State), and Dean Acheson (Under Secretary of State). The debate was thus confined to the *executive branch* of our government.

Checkpoint

1. One of the President's executive powers is to manage the foreign policy of the U.S. To what extent do you believe the President must consult with Congress before making major foreign policy decisions?

2. Are there any cases where the President should not consult with the Congress?

3. To what extent should the President listen to the public on major foreign policy decisions? Should he or she follow the wishes of the public majority even if he or she feels the public is wrong?

4. What was the extent of public debate prior to the U.S. intervention in the Persian Gulf in 1990-1991? What role did Congress play in the debate over and the execution of this war?

Chapter Three

Falling Dominoes

By 1950, the U.S. had decided to support the French colonialist presence in Vietnam with military aid. In addition, U.S. intelligence officers with the Central Intelligence Agency (CIA) began to appear in Saigon, the largest city in the south of Vietnam. Their job was to collect information on the communist influences in Vietnam.

Two overriding considerations drove U.S. policy in this period. First, the U.S. was concerned with maintaining France as an ally in Europe against the Soviets and in Asia against China. Second, the Truman Doctrine called for support of any state that was trying to defend itself against communist insurgency, that is, armed aggression designed to topple the present government. In 1948, President Harry Truman promised to send economic, and, if necessary, military aid to any nation threatened by communism.

The French sought a means of channeling Vietnamese nationalism away from the communists. They enlisted the aid of the former emperor of Vietnam, Bao Dai. Bao Dai had served twice before as a figurehead leader in the pay of first the French and then, during WWII, the Japanese. The "Bao Dai Solution", as this plan was called, created a southern state in Vietnam that was part of the French Union. Bao Dai would operate as a puppet of the French colonial government. The French hoped that this development would begin to unite anti-communists in Vietnam and transform the appearance of the war from a colonial to a civil war.

The U.S. reluctantly supported the "Bao Dai Solution", but U.S. intelligence sources as early as 1948 had recognized Ho Chi Minh as the most popular and powerful political figure in Vietnam. Nonetheless, American support of the puppet regime in the south of Vietnam appeared to be the best means available to ensure the continued support by the French of U.S. anti-communist policies in Europe and Asia.

Despite U.S. aid, French forces in Vietnam continually lost ground to the Vietminh in the early 1950's. There was little popular support in the South for the emperor and few Vietnamese were interested in supporting a political figure they saw as a collaborator. Ho Chi Minh and the Vietminh continued to improve their military and political position. France began to suffer heavy casualties in 1953 and popular support in France for the war began to wane. The willingness of the U.S. and the U.N. to accept a truce in Korea led some French leaders to call for negotiations in Vietnam.

Political considerations in the U.S. supported continued military aid to the French. In 1952, Dwight Eisenhower was elected President at least partly on the strength of a

Republican campaign that pictured the Democrats as being "soft" on communism. Democrats were said to have "lost" China to the communists through inaction in 1948. Eisenhower and his new administration did not want to be portrayed as the administration that "lost" Vietnam.

Direct military aid to the French reached record proportions in 1953. The French continued to seek a negotiated settlement but wanted very much to negotiate from a position of strength. To achieve this "position of strength," they prepared for a major set-piece (artillery and air power) battle in the valley at Dienbienphu. The French general in charge of this operation, Navarre, created an air strip and a garrison staffed with many of his best troops and equipment. The forces of the Vietminh mobilized the peasants of the area to fortify the hills around Dienbienphu with camouflaged and well dug-in artillery. Chinese support for the Vietminh became crucial at this time as the Chinese made available newer and more powerful guns. The Vietminh then became a more formidable enemy.

For nearly two months the Vietminh pounded the French garrison at Dienbienphu and on May 7, 1954, the garrison surrendered. This action, and the peace conference that followed, marked the end of the first Indochina War and the shifting of the military burden from the French to the Americans.

It should be noted that the French had called for the U.S. to provide troops and air support for the French in 1954 and many within the Eisenhower administration supported this idea. Some consideration was given to the use of tactical atomic weapons against the Vietminh forces entrenched in the hills around Dienbienphu. But these deliberations remained secret and apart from public debate. As was the case in the decision to support the French in 1946, public policy was being shaped without public information or debate.

Foreign policy constraints also limited the popularity of this proposal. Many American policy makers feared a wider war in Southeast Asia that would involve Chinese troops. Few wanted to face the possibility of confronting millions of Chinese soldiers in a land battle. The Korean War had taught the U.S. the cost of such a confrontation. Others feared the escalation of the war in Southeast Asia into a nuclear conflict. This two-headed fear of Chinese troops and Soviet nuclear bombs provided severe limitations to U.S. military options in the area for the next twenty years.

Thus, several factors came together in 1954 to persuade the French to abandon Vietnam. The military defeat at Dienbienphu, the reluctance of the U.S. to enter a wider war, the growing popularity of the Vietminh, and waning support in France forced the French to the negotiating tables in Geneva. The treaty that resulted from this conference was called the *Geneva Agreements*. The military successes of the Vietminh enabled them to negotiate from a position of strength. Still, France held an important card that had not been played, the threat of direct military intervention from the U.S. if the situation became desperate. This, along with poor economic conditions in the Soviet Union and China that weakened the Vietminh's military options, provided the French with considerable leverage at the bargaining tables.

The French wished to create a separate state in the South that could be reunited with the North after general elections sometime in the future. Military and civilian personnel were to be allowed to move freely from one section to another for a period of time. The territorial integrity of the neighboring nations of Laos and Cambodia would be maintained. Moscow and Peking pressured the Vietminh to accept these guidelines. A provisional (temporary) line at the 17th parallel marked the separation of the Democratic Republic of Vietnam (DRV) in the north from the State of Vietnam (SVN) in the south. Within two years of the date of the agreement, elections would be held to unite the two countries. Of the nine countries that attended the conference, only four, the Soviet Union, China, Britain, and France, signed the agreement. Significantly absent from the final agreement were the regime in South Vietnam and the U.S.

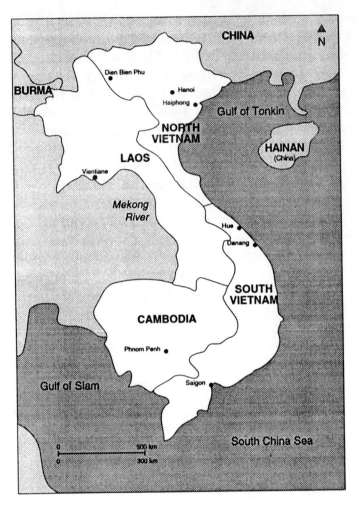

Vietnam as divided at the 17th parallel in 1954 by the Geneva Agreements.

An artificial country had been created in the south to cover the French withdrawal from Indochina and to facilitate an increased American presence. The U.S. moved quickly to increase its commitments to South Vietnam.

This move was based on a concept that President Eisenhower made public in a press conference in April of 1954. In the passage that follows Eisenhower describes the *Domino Principle*. As you read the text of the speech, keep in mind that not all interests of a country are spoken in public. These private interests are often difficult to see, but they frequently help dictate public policy. Try to answer the following questions after you read the speech.

Checkpoint

1. What three justifications does Eisenhower give for U.S. interests in Vietnam?

2. What countries does Eisenhower see falling as a result of the domino effect?

3. To what is Eisenhower alluding when he says "Asia ... has already lost some 450 million of its peoples to the Communist dictatorships"?

4. Were there any private, unspoken interests of the U.S. in the area that Eisenhower did not mention?

5. Did the U.S. speak freely and openly of all of its interests in the Mideast in the 1991 Persian Gulf War? Why are some interests purposefully not mentioned?

6. Why was it so important to the French to change the appearance of the war from a colonial war of independence to a civil war of national survival? In forming your answer, think of the differences between the American Revolutionary War and the Civil War.

Q: Robert Richards, Copley Press: Mr. President, would you mind commenting on the strategic importance of Indochina to the free world? I think there has been, across the country, some lack of understanding of just what it means to us.

THE PRESIDENT: You have, of course, both the specific and the general when you talk about these things.

First of all, you have the specific value of a locality in its production of materials that the world needs.

Then you have the possibility that many human beings pass under a dictatorship that is inimical to the free world.

Finally, you have broader considerations that might follow what you would call the "falling domino" principle. You have a row of dominoes set up, you knock over the first one, and what will happen to the last one is certainty that it will go over very quickly. So you could have a beginning of a disintegration that would have the most profound influences.

Now, with respect to the first one, two of the items from this particular area that the world uses are tin and tungsten. They are very important. There are others, of course, the rubber plantations and so on.

Then with respect to more people passing under this domination, Asia, after all, has already lost some 450 million of its people to the Communist dictatorship, and we simply can't afford greater losses.

But when we come to the possible sequence of events, the loss of Indochina, of Burma, of Thailand, of the Peninsula, and Indonesia following, now you begin to talk about areas that not only multiply the disadvantages that you would suffer through loss of materials, sources of materials, but now you are talking really about millions and millions and millions of people.

Finally, the geographical position achieved thereby does many things. It turns the so-called island defensive chain of Japan, Formosa, of the Philippines and to the southward; it moves in to threaten Australia and New Zealand.

It takes away, in its economic aspects, that region that Japan must have as a trading area or Japan, in turn, will have

37

only one place in the world to go -- that is, towards the Communist areas in order to live.

So, the possible consequences of the loss are just incalculable to the free world....

Chapter Four

Intervention

After the Geneva Agreements were signed in 1954, a period of 300 days was designated as a time when the Vietnamese could move freely between the two Vietnams. Nearly one million people moved to the South as a result of encouragement from the U.S., primarily through Church leaders. Over 100,000 Vietnamese chose to move north into communist Vietnam. The U.S. and France interpreted these events as a signal that most Vietnamese politically favored the new state in the South and opposed the communist dictatorship in the North. In truth, most of the immigrants to the South were Catholics who wanted to stay as close as possible to the remnants of the French empire with which they had collaborated. They feared reprisals from the new communist government.

A leader had to be found in the South; a leader of sufficient stature to counter the powerful and charismatic Ho in the North. The U.S. initially chose to back, with some reluctance, a Catholic Vietnamese called Ngo Dinh Diem. As U.S. intervention increased, that reluctant support would turn to enthusiastic support.

Diem had some of the attributes the U.S. was looking for in a leader. He was a Catholic and would gain support from the politically powerful Catholic minority. He was a staunch anti-communist willing to support U.S. aims of containment and democracy. He had not collaborated with the French. On the negative side, he was an aristocrat with no ability to identify with the peasantry. He was cool, aloof and insensitive to the needs of the general population. But during a three year stay in the U.S. in the early 50's, Diem had managed to convince some important American religious and political leaders that he was the best choice to lead South Vietnam. He was seen as the only person capable of off-setting the popularity of Ho. Most importantly for U.S. policy makers, he was pliable and would support U.S. intervention in Vietnam.

The U.S. hoped to have found in Diem a leader who would support the policy of containment and prove to be a magnetic leader who could establish a democracy in the South. Vietnam was to be a showcase of American foreign policy. However, from the time of his rigged election in 1955 to his assassination in 1963, Diem was not the leader the U.S. had pictured as leading South Vietnam to democracy and self-sufficiency. He was politically ruthless, frequently buying off his enemies, or, if that failed, having them assassinated. He alienated large segments of the population through disastrous attempts at land reform. He openly favored fellow Catholics (about 10% of the population) by giving them key positions in government, thus alienating the Buddhist majority. The only political base he succeeded in building was through the landlords, the Catholics, and the army. He resisted U.S. advice to compromise and increase civil liberties. He censored the press and arrested Vietminh sympathizers without formal charges. He surrounded himself with the only advisers he could trust, his family. Though "elected" to the Presidency, Diem was as ruthless a dictator as Vietnam had ever seen. In 1963 he was assassinated in a coup of generals from his own army. The U.S. supported the coup. Whether the U.S. supported the actual assassination is unclear.

Fervent anti-communism in the 1950's in America had helped shape a foreign policy that saw Diem as the only hope in South Vietnam. The U.S. pictured communism as monolithic in nature, that all communist nations received direction from Moscow. The communist world was seen as one entity bent on world domination. This entity, as the U.S. saw it, revolved on a Moscow-Hanoi-Peking axis that was determined to conquer and subjugate all of Vietnam.

To battle this perceived threat, the U.S. entered into a military alliance known as the Southeast Asia Treaty Organization. Included in SEATO were the U.S., Great Britain, France, Australia, New Zealand, the Philippines, Thailand, and Pakistan. Cambodia, Laos, and South Vietnam were also under the protective "umbrella" of SEATO. This organization would, in time, provide the U.S. with legal authority to supply military aid and advisers to South Vietnam. The story of the ratification of this treaty in the U.S. Senate is an important case study in public policy formation.

The SEATO treaty as presented to the Senate consisted of two parts. The first dealt with outside aggression and obliged the signatories to come to the defense of a member attacked by a foreign nation. The Senate had no problem with this part of the treaty since the U.S. was already party to a similar treaty in the North Atlantic Treaty

Organization (NATO).

The second part of the treaty was more worrisome. The second provision called for the members of SEATO to consult whenever a member nation was threatened with internal insurrection. Secretary of State John Foster Dulles assured the Senate that this provision authorized consultation only and could not be used to justify armed intervention in the event of a civil war. The treaty was approved by the Senate. What the Senate did not realize was the importance of defining "outside aggression". Who would make that decision as to whether a situation consisted of outside aggression or internal subversion? In the years that followed, the President and his advisers would make that decision. And that decision would lead the U.S. down the path of an undeclared war.

The advisers the U.S. sent to Vietnam trained and organized the South Vietnamese Army to prepare for armed aggression from the North. It is clear that as early as 1954, the U.S. saw an approaching military conflict in Vietnam. It is also clear that the U.S. saw the coming war as an international struggle involving two distinct countries, North and South Vietnam. Those in the North saw the struggle as a civil war, much like the American Civil War, a struggle for reunification. As we shall see, this difference in perception contributed greatly to the failure of U.S. policy in Vietnam.

Diem solidified his position with the support of the CIA. Colonel Edward Lansdale was given the mission of "teaching" Diem his job. Lansdale provided U.S. funds to bribe Vietnamese officials to support the new premier. This covert activity was at the direction of the executive branch and without the knowledge of Congress or the American people. Again, public policy was being shaped without public debate or knowledge.

While Diem was strengthening his position, communists in South Vietnam began to form into political and military organizations like the People's Liberation Armed Front (PLAF) and the National Liberation Front (NLF). These groups provided the pressure for change in the South. During the late 1950's, these groups saw the struggle in the South as primarily political. It was hoped that popular discontent in the South with Diem would lead to a general uprising that would catapult communists to power and reunify the country. The Communist Party in Hanoi supported cadres (small, secret groups of South Vietnamese) that carried out a limited campaign of political and military pressure in the South. These cadres were reluctant to provoke the U.S. into taking a larger part in military operations in Vietnam. But, by 1963, the U.S. had dramatically increased its commitment to South Vietnam. As the U.S. increased its commitment, the PLAF and the NLF increased their military activities and Vietnam found itself, once again, fully immersed in war.

In 1961, John F. Kennedy (JFK) gained the Presidency. Though he was a fervent anti-communist and a believer in containment, JFK saw the U.S. commitment in Vietnam in terms of nation building, creating a democratic showplace in Southeast Asia. U.S. policy had been challenged by the Soviet Union in many areas around the world including Cuba and Berlin. JFK saw Vietnam as another challenge. Reeling from the Bay of Pigs disaster of 1962 in which the U.S. backed an ill-prepared coup attempt by Cuban nationals, JFK was intent on nation building in Vietnam.

43

He chose to increase military aid to South Vietnam. In a fateful decision of U.S. intervention, JFK decided to drastically increase the number of advisers from 800 to 16,000. Again, this was a decision far removed from public debate and Congressional sanction. The North saw this as clear evidence of a U.S. policy designed to escalate the war.

In the interview that follows, JFK is questioned by two of the most important journalists of the day, Chet Huntley and David Brinkley. He reiterates U.S. belief in the Domino Theory but targets China as the major threat in Southeast Asia.

John F. Kennedy, Transcript of Broadcast on NBC's "Huntley-Brinkley Report," September 9, 1963.

MR. HUNTLEY: Mr. President, in respect to our difficulties in South Viet-Nam, could it be that our Government tends occasionally to get locked into a policy or an attitude and then finds it difficult to alter or shift that policy?

THE PRESIDENT: Yes, that is true. I think in the case of South Viet-Nam we have been dealing with a government which is in control, has been in control for 10 years. In addition, we have felt for the last 2 years that the struggle against the Communists was going better. Since June, however, the difficulties with the Buddhists, we have been concerned about a deterioration, particularly in the Saigon area, which hasn't been felt greatly in the outlying areas but may spread. So we are faced with the problem of wanting to protect the area against the Communists. On the other hand, we have to deal with the government there. That produces a kind of ambivalence in our efforts which exposes us to some criticism. We are using our influence to persuade the government there to take those steps which will win back support. That takes some time and we must be patient, we

44

must persist.

MR. HUNTLEY: Are we likely to reduce our aid to South Viet-Nam now?

THE PRESIDENT: I don't think that would be helpful at this time. If you reduce your aid, it is possible you could have some effect upon the government structure there. On the other hand, you might have a situation which could bring about a collapse. Strongly in our minds is what happened in the case of China at the end of World War II, where China was lost, a weak government became increasingly unable to control events. We don't want that.

MR. BRINKLEY: Mr. President, have you had any reason to doubt this so-called "domino theory," that if South Viet-Nam falls, the rest of southeast Asia will go behind it?

THE PRESIDENT: No, I believe it. I believe it. I think the struggle is close enough. China is so large, looms so high just beyond the frontiers, that if South Viet-Nam went, it would not only give them an improved geographic position for a guerrilla assault on Malaya, but would also give the impression that the wave of the future in southeast Asia was China and the Communists. So I believe it.

In May of 1963, a Buddhist monk, Thich Quang Duc, was doused with gasoline by two assistants as he sat in a street in Saigon. As passers-by and the press looked on, Quang Duc set himself afire in protest of Diem's policies that discriminated against Buddhists. His death by self-immolation was one of the most compelling visual images of the Vietnam War. His martyrdom foreshadowed the death of Diem and his policies just seven months later. In a coup of generals, Diem was replaced by military leaders Minh, Don, and Khiem. They would remain in

45

office as long as they cooperated with the U.S.

As the military commitment increased, the U.S. was pulled into a quagmire that would sap much of its political, economic, and moral strength in the next decade. The challenge for policy makers was to fully assess the costs and benefits of U.S. policy in Southeast Asia. But in assessing those costs, they frequently refused to question the underlying assumptions driving those policies.

Checkpoint

1. What fundamental beliefs or assumptions shaped U.S. foreign policy in Southeast Asia in the 1950's?

2. How and why had those beliefs changed by 1964?

3. What goals did each of the following players have in Vietnam during 1963?

   . U.S. government

   . NLF

   . Buddhists

   . Communist Party Central Committee (Hanoi)

4. What fateful decision did JFK make? Might that decision have been different if it had been opened to public debate? Did JFK need Congressional approval for this action?

Chapter Five

A Basis for War

By the middle of 1964, it was clear that the war against communist insurgency in the South was not going well. Forces of the NLF and PLAF were making steady gains in rural areas, though urban areas remained under the control of the South Vietnamese Army of the Republic of Vietnam, (ARVN). It was also clear that the new government of generals that followed Diem was ineffective and lacked popular support. American military commanders warned that without increased U.S.support, the government of South Vietnam would collapse. The new President, Lyndon Baines Johnson (LBJ), did not want to appear weak in facing the communist foe in Vietnam. Johnson would face an election challenge in 1964 and he clearly remembered the charges of "losing China" that were leveled against the Democrats in the election of 1952. The stage was set for increasing U.S. intervention.

The military, encouraged by Johnson and his advisers, began to search for an incident that would elicit broad popular support for a widening of the war. On August 2nd and 4th, two incidents occurred in the sea off North

Vietnam that would provide the only legal basis for the increasing U.S. presence in Vietnam over the following five years. The U.S. destroyers, *Maddox* and *Turner Joy*, were collecting intelligence information in the Gulf of Tonkin in support of South Vietnamese naval operations in the area. On August 2nd, a lone North Vietnamese gunboat fired on one of the destroyers which was hit by a single bullet. Two days later, military reports detailed a further attack by North Vietnamese gunboats on both destroyers. A subsequent Congressional investigation in 1968 began to raise questions about the accuracy of these reports. As more documents have become available through declassification, historians now believe that the second attack was a fabrication based upon poor use of radar and overanxious crews on both ships. It now appears that the military made false and incomplete reports of the action known as the Gulf of Tonkin Incident.

President Johnson seized on the incident to ask Congress for broad powers to retaliate against the "unprovoked attacks" against the two American destroyers. The Gulf of Tonkin Resolution provided LBJ with a "blank check", virtually unlimited freedom, to respond to North Vietnamese threats or aggression. The President was given the power to fight an undeclared war with Congressional backing. Only two Senators, Morse and Gruening, voted against the resolution. The reading that follows is the text of the famous Gulf of Tonkin Resolution. Try to answer the following questions as you read the text.

Checkpoint

1. Assess the statement in the third paragraph, "the United States ... has no territorial, military, or political ambitions in that area." Do you agree with the statement? Why or why not?

2. Identify the words or phrases that made the resolution a blank check for LBJ.

3. What is the purpose of mentioning SEATO and the UN in section 2?

4. Compare the Vietnam War with the Persian Gulf War from the stand point of Presidential powers. In both cases, war was waged without a formal Declaration of War from Congress. Why, in your opinion, did the U.S. stop short of this formal declaration in both cases? Do you believe the President was given too much power in the Vietnam War? In the Persian Gulf War? If you believe differently about Presidential powers in the two wars, what explains that difference?

51

The Gulf of Tonkin Resolution

1964

To promote the maintenance of international peace and security in southeast Asia.

Whereas naval units of the Communist regime in Vietnam, in violation of the principles of the Charter of the United Nations and of international law, have deliberately and repeatedly attacked United States naval vessels lawfully present in international waters, and have thereby created a serious threat to international peace; and

Whereas these attacks are part of a deliberate and systematic campaign of aggression that the Communist regime in North Vietnam has been waging against its neighbors and the nations joined with them in the collective defense of their freedom; and

Whereas the United States is assisting the peoples of southeast Asia to protect their freedom and has no territorial, military or political ambitions in that area, but desires only that these peoples should be left in peace to work out their own destinies in their own way: Now, therefore, be it *Resolved by the Senate and House of Representatives of the United States of America in Congress assembled,* That the Congress approves and supports the determination of the President, as Commander in Chief, to take all necessary measures to repel any armed attack against the forces of the United States and to prevent further aggression.

SEC. 2. The United States regards as vital to its national interest and to world peace the maintenance of international peace and security in southeast Asia. Consonant with the Constitution of the United States and the Charter of the United Nations and in accordance with its obligations under the Southeast Asia Collective Defense Treaty, the United States is, therefore, prepared, as the President determines, to take all necessary steps, including the use of armed force, to assist any member or protocol state of the Southeast Asia Collective Defense Treaty requesting assistance in defense of its freedom.

SEC. 3. This resolution shall expire when the President shall determine that the peace and security of the area is reasonably assured by international conditions created by action of the United Nations or otherwise, except that it may be terminated earlier by concurrent resolution of the Congress.

Retaliation and Escalation

The U.S. launched air strikes against the North in retaliation for the Gulf of Tonkin incident. North Vietnam increased the tension by, for the first time, sending one of its well-trained and well-equipped regular army units into the South. These troops, the Peoples Army of Vietnam (PAVN), were used to mount attacks against U.S. air bases in the South. Such attacks gave LBJ further excuses to widen the war, as we shall see in the next chapter.

Before we look at the means of escalation, we must first examine two additional factors that influenced the decisions that broadened the scope of the war. In 1964, LBJ faced an election challenge from Senator Barry Goldwater. Goldwater backed the Gulf of Tonkin Resolution but was more "hawkish" (aggressive) in his calls for increased military intervention. He even intimated that as President he would consider the use of nuclear weapons in Vietnam. As a result, LBJ could not afford to be labeled as soft on communism. Such a label would seriously hurt his election chances. At the same time, he wanted to be seen as the "peace candidate," pledging to keep this an Asian war fought by Asian soldiers.

Another factor, this one internal to Vietnam, also

spurred LBJ into escalation. This factor was the continued lack of leadership in South Vietnam. In another coup, General Minh was overthrown by General Khanh who became the political leader of the South in 1964. But like his predecessors, he lacked broad popular support and was seen by the South Vietnamese as a lackey to the U.S. presence.

Responding to popular pressure to reach an accommodation with the North, Khanh began to urge negotiations with the North Vietnamese. This was inconsistent with U.S. policy. The U.S. was convinced in 1964 that any free elections would result in a neutralist vote that would lead to the end of U.S. influence in Vietnam. Worse yet, the path would then be clear for reunification. Thus the U.S. continued to follow a policy that ignored the wishes of the Vietnamese people. Though trying to build a democratic nation in South Vietnam, the U.S. followed a policy that ignored the ballot box.

LBJ hoped that the expression of Congressional support in the Gulf of Tonkin Resolution would help sway popular opinion in the South toward an increasing U.S. role. It is unclear whether in 1964 LBJ saw that expanded role as limited to air power or as including the use of American ground troops. In the speech that follows, LBJ defends a limited role in Vietnam, a position opposed by hawks like Nixon and Rockefeller. (Note: When LBJ uses the phrase "going north in Vietnam", he is referring to an invasion of the North using U.S. ground troops.) Consider these questions as you read LBJ's speech:

Checkpoint

1. In the second and third paragraphs, LBJ uses the phrases, "only as a last resort", "so just for the moment", and "at this stage of the game". Why did he include these phrases? What do these phrases say about this speech?

2. What public interests does LBJ raise in this speech ?

3. What private interests of the U.S. are left unsaid?

4. To what is he referring in the last line when he talks about "start(ing) a war " and "prevent(ing) one"?

Lyndon B. Johnson, Public Address, Manchester, New Hampshire, September 28, 1964.

Some of our people -- Mr. Nixon, Mr. Rockefeller, Mr. Scranton, and Mr. Goldwater -- have all, at some time or other, suggested the possible wisdom of going north in Vietnam. Well, now, before you start attacking someone and you launch a big offensive, you better give some consideration to how you are going to protect what you have. And when the brigadier general can walk down the streets of Saigon, as they did the other day, and take over the police station, the radio station, and the government without firing a shot, I don't know how much offensive we are prepared to launch.

As far as I am concerned, I want to be very cautious and careful, and use it *only as a last resort*, when I start dropping bombs around that are likely to involve American boys in a

55

war in Asia with 700 million Chinese.

So *just for the moment* I have not thought we were ready for American boys to do the fighting for Asian boys. What I have been trying to do, with the situation that I found, was to get the boys in Vietnam to do their own fighting with our advice and with our equipment....We are not going north and drop bombs *at this stage of the game*, and we are not going south and run out and leave it for the Communists to take over.

Now we have lost 190 American lives, and to each one of those 190 families this is a major war....I often wake up in the night and think about how many I could lose if I made a misstep.

When we retaliated in the Tonkin Gulf, we dropped bombs in their nests where they had their PT boats housed, and we dropped them within thirty-five miles of the Chinese border. I don't know what you would think if they started dropping them thirty-five miles from your border, but I think that is something you have to take into consideration.

So....we are going to continue to try and get them to save their own freedom....We think that losing 190 lives in the period that we have been out there is bad. But it is not like 190,000 that we might lose the first month if we escalated that war.

....We are trying somehow to evolve a way, as we have in some other places, where the North Vietnamese and the Chinese Communists will finally, after getting worn down, conclude that they will leave their neighbors alone. And if they do, we will come home tomorrow.

It is not any problem to start a war....I know some folks that I think could start one mighty easy. But it is a pretty difficult problem for us to prevent one, and that is what we are trying to do.

Chapter Six

Americanizing the War

The year 1965 marked some decisive changes in the players and the conduct of the war. General Khanh had been ousted in a U.S. condoned military coup, because of his attempts to negotiate with the communists. He had been replaced by Air Vice-Marshal Ky and General Thieu. General William Westmoreland became commander of U.S. forces in Vietnam. LBJ had been overwhelmingly elected to his own term as President. These players were committed to a military victory in Vietnam.

President Johnson was deliberately ambiguous in his speeches in 1964. He wished to keep the U.S. commitment limited to air support for and advisers to the ARVN forces. But by 1965, there were 82,000 American troops in Vietnam and by 1968, a half million. What factors led to this dramatic escalation and in what ways did the U.S. escalate the war?

Publicly, LBJ professed to be committed, in 1965, to the building of a viable, democratic, and eventually, self-sufficient state in South Vietnam. This government, resting on popular support, would use U.S. aid and advisers to create a stable haven of anti-communism in the South consistent with America's vision of containment. However, a succession of South Vietnamese leaders had failed to gain the much needed support of the South Vietnamese people. The Johnson administration maintained that containment and the building of a democratic South were still unrealized goals and, therefore, two of the arguments in favor of escalation.

Another factor was the growing power and prestige of the Communists in the South. The NLF and the PLAF continued to enjoy widespread military and popular success in the South. The South Vietnamese military estimated that nearly 75% of the rural areas in the South were under communist control in 1965. Men and munitions continued to stream south across the Ho Chi Minh trail, the major conduit for men and supplies moving from north to south. ARVN forces were suffering high rates of desertion as a result of disastrous defeats at the hands of the NLF and factionalism in its leadership. The plan to train and equip the South Vietnamese to fight on their own was in shambles. Military advisers in the U.S. and Vietnam predicted the collapse of Southern military forces if the U.S. did not intervene with an increased military commitment.

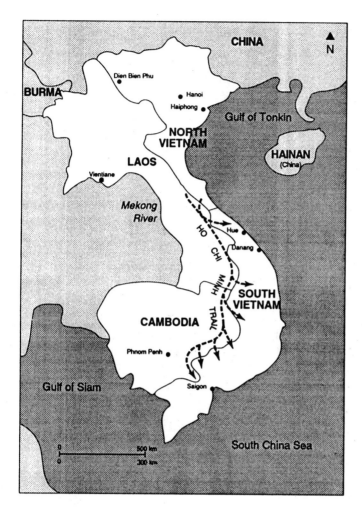

Ho Chi Minh Trail, Major Supply Route used by North Vietnam.

The final, and overriding reason for escalation, was credibility. One adviser to Defense Secretary McNamara, John McNaughton, wrote that 70% of the reason for being in Vietnam was maintaining credibility as a superpower on the world stage. A loss in Vietnam, it was argued, would so damage the reputation of the U.S. that communists would be emboldened to press the struggle for worldwide domination on a much larger scale. The military called for an increased level of arms and men in Vietnam to prevent the collapse of South Vietnam. Thus, in 1965, another fateful decision loomed. Would the U.S. escalate its commitment in defense of South Vietnam?

Acting on the "blank check" of the Gulf of Tonkin Resolution, LBJ had ordered a series of retaliatory bombing raids in late 1964 and early 1965. Key advisers such as McNamara and McGeorge Bundy, Special Assistant for National Security Affairs, urged the President to initiate a sustained bombing campaign designed to shore up the failing South Vietnamese government and military. In February, without consulting Congress or opening the question to public debate, LBJ began Operation Rolling Thunder. This operation entailed the sustained bombing of targets in Vietnam. The bombing of Vietnam would total 17 million tons of bombs or three times the amount used in World War II. Twenty million bomb craters would be created. Millions of Vietnamese citizens would be killed or wounded by the bombing. But again, this public policy was not open to public debate. It was the decision of a small group of advisers and the President.

Escalation was met with escalation. For the first time, well-trained and well-equipped units of the North Vietnamese regular army, PAVN, entered the South. These troops did not rely on the ambush and booby trap methods of the NLF. They were trained to fight effectively in set-piece battles and were more than a match for the ARVN. The forces of PAVN and the NLF began to attack

U.S. airbases, and the military pointed out the need for American ground troops to secure the areas around these bases. As a result of a directive from the President, Marines were dispatched to protect U.S. airbases. But by June of 1965, it was clear that despite U.S. bombing and increased ground forces, the communists were still winning the war. The military called upon the President to commit offensive ground forces to the war in Vietnam. Another fateful decision loomed.

Members of Congress were aware of the deteriorating situation in Vietnam and approached the President with their concerns. Some urged the increased use of American troops. A few favored withdrawal. Others, like Senator Mike Mansfield, wanted an increased but limited commitment. Within the inner circle of Presidential advisers, Under Secretary of State George Ball warned the President to abandon Vietnam or suffer a protracted and costly war. Ball, in retrospect, provided the best analysis of the situation and an almost prophetic vision of the costs that the U.S. would incur. He, among the close Presidential advisers, seemed to stand alone in his recommendation to withdraw and avoid further escalation. In the passage that follows, George Ball attempts to explain to the President a way out of the situation in Vietnam. His perception of credibility seems to differ from that of the President and the President's other advisers.

The following passage is excerpted from the July 21, 1965 meeting of LBJ and his military advisers.

BALL: Mr. President, I can foresee a perilous voyage, very dangerous. I have great and grave apprehensions that we can win under these conditions.

PRESIDENT: But George, is there another course in the national interest, some course that is better than the one McNamara proposes [escalation]? We know it is dangerous and perilous, but the big question is, can it be avoided?

BALL: There is no course that will allow us to cut our losses. If we get bogged down, our cost might be substantially greater. The pressures to create a larger war would be irresistible.

PRESIDENT: Tell me then, what other road can I go?

BALL: Take what precautions we can, Mr. President. Take our losses, let their government fall apart, negotiate, discuss, knowing full well there will be a probable take-over by the Communists.

Later that day, the President and his advisers again met and discussed credibility.

BALL: We cannot win Mr. President. This war will be long and protracted. The most we can hope for is a messy conclusion. There remains a great danger of intrusion by the Chinese. But the biggest problem is the problem of the long war.

PRESIDENT: This is important. Can Westerners, in the absence of accurate intelligence, successfully fight Asians in jungle rice paddies?

BALL: I think we have all underestimated the seriousness of this situation. I think a long, protracted war will disclose our weakness, our strength.

George McT. Kahin, *Intervention: How America Became Involved in Vietnam,* (Garden City, NY: Anchor Books, 1987), pp. 370-376.

Ball then goes on to describe a plan that would force the South Vietnamese to ask the Americans to leave. A series of impossible demands placed on the South Vietnamese by the U.S would so strain relations that South Vietnam would no longer want U.S. support. The country would then fall into communist hands but only *after* the U.S. had been asked to leave. This plan was designed to help the U.S. "save face" in withdrawal.

The President replies to Ball's ideas:

PRESIDENT: But George, wouldn't all these countries say that Uncle Sam was a paper tiger, wouldn't we lose credibility breaking the word of three presidents, if we did as you have proposed? It would seem to be an irreparable blow. But I gather you don't think so.

BALL: No sir. The worse blow would be that the mightiest power on earth is unable to defeat a handful of guerillas.

The rest of LBJ's advisers were nearly unanimous in desiring escalation. For them, credibility was essential to the U.S. They shared a belief in the winnability of the war. None could conceive of a realistic threat from the communists. For Johnson, the cost of withdrawal was too high; he would not be remembered as the president who lost Vietnam and broke the promises of Eisenhower and Kennedy. A few days later, LBJ presents his assessment of the options.

Checkpoint

1. Another fateful decision was made in these July meetings. Why weren't these issues aired publicly? Why were the discussions limited to the President and his advisers?

2. Why does the President choose option e. over option d.? What does this say about the formation of public policy on the war?

LBJ's Options

THE PRESIDENT: The situation in Vietnam is deteriorating. Even though we now have 80 to 90,000 men there, the situation is not very safe. We have these choices:

    a. Use our massive power, including SAC [Strategic Air Command] to bring the enemy to his knees. Less than 10% of our people urge this course of action. [Presumably implicit in this course of action would be a willingness to resort to nuclear warfare.]

    b. We could get out, on the grounds that we don't belong there. Not very many people feel that this is the way about Vietnam. Most feel that our national honor is at stake and that we must keep our commitments there.

    c. We could keep our forces at the present level,

George, McT. Kahin, *Intervention: How America Became Involved in Vietnam,* (Garden City, NY: Anchor Books, 1987), p. 393.

64

approximately 80,000 men, but suffer the consequences of losing additional territory and of accepting increased casualties. We could "hunker up." No one is recommending this course.

d. We could ask for everything we might desire from Congress -- money, authority to call up the reserves, acceptance of the deployment of more combat battalions. This dramatic course of action would involve declaring a state of emergency and a request for several billion dollars. Many favor this course. However, if we do go all out in this fashion, Hanoi would be able to ask the Chinese Communists and the Soviets to increase aid and add to their existing commitments.

e. We have chosen to do what is necessary to meet the present situation, but not to be unnecessarily provocative to either the Russians or the Communist Chinese. We will give the commanders the men they say they need and, out of existing material in the U.S., we will give them the material they say they need. We will get the necessary money in the new budget and will use our transfer authority until January. We will neither brag about what we are doing [nor] thunder at the Chinese Communists and the Russians.

It should be noted that, at this point, no attempts were made to negotiate an end to the war. Negotiation, in the eyes of the U.S., was just a prelude to surrender. Certainly, it was thought, a fourth-rate power like North Vietnam could not withstand a dedicated effort by the most powerful nation on Earth.

Assessing the Decisions of 1965

The first of the two fateful decisions of 1965 was the decision to dramatically escalate the bombing of North Vietnam. Rolling Thunder had serious implications for the U.S., both in the domestic, as well as the international

65

political arenas. At home, Rolling Thunder helped unite and gain additional support for the still small anti-war movement. Internationally, the bombing moved the U.S. closer to the much-feared wider war that could involve the Soviets or the Chinese. Rolling Thunder was an excellent example of the arrogance of power that filled the U.S. military in Vietnam; the belief that massive American firepower could defeat any enemy. Much of Operation Rolling Thunder was directed at the Ho Chi Minh Trail. Huge B-52 bombers "carpeted" the trail with bombs targeted for bridges, roads, and material. The bombing proved ineffective as the North Vietnamese quickly rebuilt or merely went around bombed areas.

Rolling Thunder was supposed to destroy the enemy psychologically. The bombing of the North was designed to eliminate production sites and military bases. However, history (prior to the Persian Gulf War) tells us that sustained bombing is ineffective in both cases. Bombing tends to "steel" (harden) the will of a people. This was true of both the British and the Germans in WWII and proved to be true also of the North Vietnamese. History also tells us that Germany actually increased its weapon production during the intense Allied bombing. The bombing of North Vietnam was even less successful since the North was an agricultural, not an industrial, society. They were not manufacturing weapons as Germany had, but were importing them from China and the Soviet Union.

The second major military move by the U.S. in 1965 was the commitment of ground troops. This move was supposed to remove any doubt of America's resolve in supporting the South. These troops were equipped with modern weapons designed to remove any advantage the enemy enjoyed in guerilla warfare. Weapons included helicopter gunships, a new, fully automatic rifle called the M-16, night scopes and infrared spotters to amplify night vision, and herbicides that could defoliate (remove the leaves from growing trees and plants) large sections of jungle thereby reducing the enemy's cover.

The U.S. firmly believed in the efficacy of technology. Communist guerilla forces, on the other hand, used tactics such as booby traps, hit and run battle techniques, and assassination against pro-U.S. village leaders. The PAVN units that entered the war in 1965 were better equipped to meet U.S. and ARVN forces in set-piece battles. They were well supplied with modern Soviet and Chinese weapons.

As U.S. forces grew in 1965 so did casualties on both sides. General Westmoreland's strategy rested on two points, mobility and firepower. "Search and destroy" missions cleared huge sections of the countryside during the day but at night the communist forces came out of hiding and retook the villages. Massive doses of firepower yielded favorable "kill ratios" (the proportion of Communist vs. Allied deaths). These kill ratios became the only means of assessing success in the war.

As fighting intensified, President Johnson felt compelled to clearly spell out why the U.S. was engaged in military operations in Vietnam and what the military and political objectives were. In a speech at Johns Hopkins University on April 7, 1965, Johnson made clear his objectives for "peace without conquest." Consider the following questions while you read the speech:

Checkpoint

1. In the introductory paragraph, what seems to be the most important reason for the U.S. presence in Vietnam? Why doesn't LBJ mention the question of credibility?

2. Johnson states, "The confused nature of this conflict cannot mask the fact that it is the new face of an old enemy." To what enemy is he referring?

3. What three reasons does LBJ give for "Why We Fight"? What historical lessons form the basis for his reasons?

4. The key concern of the North was always the reunification of the country. How does LBJ address this issue (if at all)? In his eyes, what is the nature of this conflict, a civil war or a war between nations?

5. Critics have argued that this speech was designed more to silence opposition at home than to provide a basis for a negotiated settlement. Based on the reading, with which interpretation do you agree? Why?

Lyndon B. Johnson, Address at Johns Hopkins University: "Peace Without Conquest," April 7, 1965.

...I have come here to review once again with my own people the views of the American Government.

Tonight Americans and Asians are dying for a world where each people may choose its own path to change.

This is the principle for which our ancestors fought in the valleys of Pennsylvania. It is the principle for which our sons fight for tonight in the jungles of Viet-Nam.

Viet-Nam is far away from this quiet campus. We have no territory there, nor do we seek any. The war is dirty and brutal and difficult. And some 400 young men, born into an America that is bursting with opportunity and promise, have ended their lives on Viet-Nam's steaming soil.

Why must we take this painful road?

Why must this nation hazard its ease, and its interest, and its power for the sake of people so far away?

We fight because we must fight if we are to live in a world where every country can shape its own destiny. And only in such a world will our own freedom be finally secure.

This kind of world will never be built by bombs or bullets. Yet the infirmities of man are such that force must often precede reason, and the waste of war, the works of peace.

We wish that this were not so. But we must deal with the world as it is, if it is ever to be as we wish.

The world as it is in Asia is not a serene or peaceful place.

The first reality is that North Viet-Nam has attacked the independent nation of South Viet-Nam. Its object is total conquest.

Of course, some of the people of South Viet-Nam are participating in attack on their own government. But trained men and supplies, orders and arms, flow in a constant stream from north to south.

This support is the heartbeat of the war.

And it is a war of unparalleled brutality. Simple farmers are the targets of assassination and kidnapping. Women and children are strangled in the night because their men are loyal to their government. And helpless villages are ravaged by

69

sneak attacks. Large-scale raids are conducted on towns, and terror strikes in the heart of cities.

The confused nature of this conflict can not mask the fact that it is the new face of an old enemy.

Over this war -- and all Asia -- is another reality: the deepening shadow of Communist China. The rulers in Hanoi are urged on by Peking. This is a regime which has destroyed freedom in Tibet, which has attacked India, and has been condemned by the United Nations for aggression in Korea. It is a nation which is helping the forces of violence in almost every continent. The contest in Viet-Nam is part of a wider pattern of aggressive purposes.

Why are these realities our concern? Why are we in South Viet-Nam?

We are there because we have a promise to keep. Since 1954 every American President has offered support to the people of South Viet-Nam. We have helped to build, and we have helped to defend. Thus, over many years, we have made a national pledge to help South Viet-Nam defend its independence.

And I intend to keep that promise.

To dishonor that pledge, to abandon this small and brave nation to its enemies, and to the terror that must follow, would be an unforgivable wrong.

We are also there to strengthen world order. Around the globe, from Berlin to Thailand, are people whose well-being rests, in part, on the belief that they can count on us if they are attacked. To leave Viet-Nam to its fate would shake the confidence of all these people in the value of an American commitment and in the value of an American's word. The result would be increased unrest and instability, and even wider war.

We are also there because there are great stakes in the balance. Let no one think for a moment that retreat from Viet-Nam would bring an end to conflict. The battle would be renewed in one country and then another. The central lesson of our time is that the appetite of aggression is never satisfied. To withdraw from one battlefield means only to prepare for the next. We must say in southeast Asia -- as we did in Europe -- in the words of the Bible: "Hitherto shalt thou come, but no

70

further."

There are those who say that all our effort there will be futile -- that China's power is such that it is bound to dominate all southeast Asia. But there is no end to that argument until all of the nations of Asia are swallowed up.

There are those who wonder why we have a responsibility there. Well, we have it there for the same reason that we have a responsibility for the defense of Europe. World War II was fought in both Europe and Asia, and when it ended we found ourselves with the continued responsibility for the defense of freedom.

Our objective is the independence of South Viet-Nam, and its freedom from attack. We want nothing for ourselves -- only that the people of South Viet-Nam be allowed to guide their own country in their own way.

We will do everything necessary to reach that objective. And we will do only what is absolutely necessary.

In recent months attacks on South Viet-Nam were stepped up. Thus, it became necessary for us to increase our response and make more attacks by air. This is not a change of purpose. It is a change in what we believe that purpose requires.

We do this in order to slow down aggression.

We do this to increase the confidence of the brave people of South Viet-Nam who have bravely borne this brutal battle for so many years with so many casualties.

And we do this to convince the leaders of North Viet-Nam -- and all who seek to share their conquest -- of a very simple fact:

We will not be defeated.

We will not grow tired.

We will not withdraw, either openly or under the cloak of a meaningless agreement.

We know that air attacks alone will not accomplish all of these purposes. But it is our best and prayerful judgement that they are a necessary part of the surest road to peace.

We hope that peace will come swiftly. But that is in the hands of others besides ourselves. And we must be prepared for a long continued conflict. It will require patience as well as

71

bravery, the will to endure as well as the will to resist.

I wish it were possible to convince others with words of what we now find it necessary to say with guns and planes: Armed hostility is futile. Our resources are equal to any challenge. Because we fight for values and we fight for principles, rather than territory or colonies, our patience and our determination are unending.

Once this is clear, then it should also be clear that the only path for reasonable men is the path of peaceful settlement.

Such peace demands an independence of South Viet-Nam -- securely guaranteed and able to shape its own relationships to all others -- free from outside interference -- tied to no alliance -- a military base for no other country.

These are the essentials of any final settlement.

We will never be second in the search for such a peaceful settlement in Viet-Nam.

There may be many ways to this kind of peace: in discussion or negotiation with the governments concerned; in large groups or in small ones; in the reaffirmation of old agreements or their strengthening with new ones.

We have stated this position over and over again, fifty times and more, to friend and foe alike. And we remain ready, with this purpose, for unconditional discussions.

And until that bright and necessary day of peace we will try to keep conflict from spreading. We have no desire to see thousands die in battle -- Asians or Americans. We have no desire to devastate that which the people of North Viet-Nam have built with toil and sacrifice. We will use our power with restraint and with all the wisdom that we can command.

But we will use it.

This war, like most wars, is filled with terrible irony. For what do the people of North Viet-Nam want? They want what their neighbors also desire: food for hunger; health for their bodies; a chance to learn; progress for their country; and an end to the bondage of material misery. And they would fill all these things far more readily in peaceful association with others than in the endless course of battle....

Chapter Seven

The Light at the End of the Tunnel

By 1967, Allied forces in Vietnam totaled more than one million troops. These troops included forces from the U.S., South Vietnam, New Zealand, Australia, and South Korea. Massive amounts of aid continued to flow into the country and Operation Rolling Thunder was further escalated to more than 100,000 sorties (missions) in 1967. Search and destroy missions were increased to include the total destruction of communist-controlled villages and the resettlement of their populations. Bulldozers were used to destroy communist underground installations in villages such as Ben Suc.

The resettlement program and the heavier use of B-52's alienated large sections of the peasant population. Just when the U.S. was trying to win the "battle for the hearts and minds" of the Vietnamese peasants, it was instead driving those peasants further into the camp of the communists. Resettlement programs moved peasants away from their ancestral burial grounds which were often in the fields behind their huts. Most of these peasants were Buddhists and they greatly resented this move since one of the major tenets of their religion is ancestor worship.

The relocation program was symptomatic of the U.S. approach to the war that failed to show any understanding of the people of Vietnam. The alienation of the peasant helps explain one of the compelling reasons behind the failure of U.S. policy in South Vietnam. Extensive bombing of both South and North Vietnam further alienated the population. Civilian deaths became increasingly frequent with the use of napalm (bombs made from jellied gasoline), a particularly horrible weapon. In the siege of Khe Sanh alone, 60,000 tons of napalm were used. But bombing tends to be indiscriminate and some estimates placed the ratio of civilian to military deaths at two to one or even higher. Predictions were made that the U.S. would destroy the country it had come to protect.

Westmoreland's strategy of firepower plus mobility began, in 1966, to reverse the steady gains communists had made in previous years. American and Korean troops engaged in search and destroy missions and met with considerable success when they met the enemy face to face. The second part of Westmoreland's strategy called upon ARVN forces to move into and pacify the areas that allied troops had cleared. This part of his strategy was a failure. ARVN troops could not be relied upon to carry out these missions despite training and supplies from the U.S. The South Vietnamese army suffered from high rates of desertion and lack of motivation. The political ideas of Americans, such as containment and the domino theory, were vague doctrines to the Vietnamese who were much more concerned with the basic needs of life. Politics easily becomes a secondary concern in a society struggling for the fundamental necessities like food, medicine, and shelter.

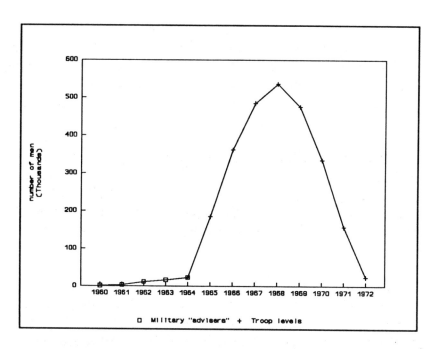

U.S. Troop Levels, 1960-1973.

The year 1967 marked the biggest American commitment to date. U.S. troops numbered 425,000. American casualties in 1967 amounted to 5,000 dead soldiers. Though communist forces were often killed in ratios of ten or fifteen to one, replacements moved in a continuous stream from the North and more than made up for casualties. The U.S. was spending $2 billion dollars per month on the war effort.

The costs of the war, in both human and monetary terms, began to erode the support of those back home in the U.S. for our war effort in Vietnam. President Johnson was trying to fight two wars at once; a war in Asia and a war against poverty at home. He refused to raise taxes to carry out his dual front war. The national debt began to soar. The anti-war movement gathered momentum with each evening news report. Vietnam was called the "livingroom war" because of the immediacy of coverage each day on the evening news. Body counts of both allied and communist forces were often the lead story in these nightly reports.

Many people began to fear a stalemate in Vietnam. A stalemate meant victory for the North. The U.S. could not afford, either militarily, economically, or politically, an endless war in Vietnam. There were many other hot spots around the world that commanded U.S. attention and resources.

Communists realized that it was only a matter of time before the U.S. realized that support of South Vietnam was a losing proposition. Their strategy was designed to weaken the resolve of the U.S. and to eliminate all other options until only one existed: withdrawal.

The year 1968, discussed in the next chapter, would mark the turning point in this struggle. The Vietnam War was to become as much a struggle for the hearts and minds of Americans as it was for the hearts and minds of the Vietnamese.

Despite the virtual stalemate on the ground, with allied victories during the day that were reversed during the night, the military projected a rosy outlook. In the reading that follows, Defense Secretary Robert McNamara reports on the progress of the war in 1967. The pacification program he refers to was an attempt to reorganize the village system of government by putting in place officials sympathetic to the U.S. and its goals. After reading this selection, try to answer the following questions.

Checkpoint

1. What adjectives would you use to describe this report? Realistic? Pessimistic? Cautious?

2. What was McNamara's purpose in this report? To whom do you think this report was addressed?

3. What part(s) of this report were aimed at the anti-war activists in the U.S. who were becoming increasingly vocal?

4. What option, in terms of the level of U.S. troop commitment, does McNamara leave open?

Defense Secretary Robert McNamara, Public Statement on Progress of the War, 1967.

On the military field, let me say to start with, the military commanders I met with -- and I met with all of the senior military commanders in the field, all of the senior Vietnamese commanders, many of the Allied commanders, Korean, and New Zealanders, for example, and many of the middle-ranking and junior U.S. officers -- all of the military commanders stated that the reports that they read in the press of military stalemate were, to use their words, the "most ridiculous statements that they had ever heard."

In their view military progress had occurred and was continuing. How did they measure this? They measured it in

77

particular by the success of what they called the large-unit actions. These are battalion-sized and larger actions.

They felt that these actions that General [William C.] Westmoreland had organized and carried on over the past several months, particularly in II and III Corps, had a spoiling effect on the Viet Cong and North Vietnamese. Before they could concentrate their troops to launch an offensive, Westmoreland, through his intelligence sources, had obtained information about the intended enemy plans and had struck the troop concentrations as they were developing, spoiling the potential of the enemy for carrying out these offensive actions.

Moreover, as you know, it has been General Westmoreland's strategy over the last several months to attack the base areas, particularly those in the II and III Corps, using B-52 strikes in some cases but in particular using a coordinated ground and air attack against these base areas to destroy the facilities, the stocks -- the recuperation areas that the Viet Cong and the North Vietnamese had used.

The military commanders felt, as a result of this contribution of spoiling attacks and attacks on the base areas, the pressure had been so great on the North Viet Cong that they had tended to shift their area of activity. Whereas up until very recently, the activity had been concentrated primarily in the II and III Corps, the offensive activities more recently -- they had moved their area of action to the I Corps.

This is understandable because in the II and III Corps -- with the loss of their base areas -- they were at the end of a very long line of communication over which their men and supplies moved from the supply centers in North Viet-Nam. This line of communications moved down the panhandle of North Viet-Nam across into Laos, down Laos to the Cambodian border, and across into South Viet-Nam -- a very, very long line of communication that was under very intense air attack, as a matter of fact.

And because this war was a handicap to them -- particularly so in connection with the strategy that Westmoreland was carrying out against them -- they shifted their area of activity to I Corps.

This accounts for their military actions there in the past several weeks. Now they have the advantage of short lines of communications extending down to the southern border of Viet-Nam, very close to the point where the troops are now very active.

Perhaps the most dramatic change that I saw that reflects the military situation was the opening of the roads.

Highway No. 1, which is the coastal route that runs from the 17th parallel -- the line of demarcation between North Viet-Nam and South Viet-Nam -- clear south to Saigon, has been broken for many, many months in literally hundreds of places, and traffic on the route has been minimal.

But within the past several months, as a result of these military actions -- planned and carried out by free-world forces -- that route has gradually been reopened in large segments.

As a matter of fact, day before yesterday, the route from the southern border of the II Corps up to Dong Hai, which is very close to the DMZ -- just a few miles south of the DMZ -- was opened for traffic.

There will continue to be ambushes, I presume, and Viet Cong strikes against it, but as I flew over the road after this long stretch was opened, literally hundreds of bicycles and scores of cars and trucks -- civilian cars and trucks -- were using it.

The same thing is true of many of the feeder roads in the III and IV Corps -- roads that are of more importance to move vegetables or rice to market or otherwise serving as an underpinning of the day-to-day life of society.

I don't want to exaggerate this or imply all roads are open -- far from it. I don't even what to suggest that many of the roads being used can be used freely night and day. They can't. But there has been a very, very noticeable -- when I say "noticeable," I mean one flying over the area can notice a very substantial increase in the number of miles of roads that are open to traffic and the volume of traffic on the roads.

Perhaps a word about the air operations is in order.

We have suffered materially in air operations because of night vision -- the difficulty of acquiring targets at night.

There have been some very significant changes in technology. I don't want to go into the details of them other than to say they have greatly increased the capability of our forces to carry on all-weather attacks on the lines of communication, both in South Viet-Nam and in North Viet-Nam.

These, in conjunction with new weapons, new types of ordinance, that have been designed and developed in recent years and brought into production in recent months in combination have increased the effectiveness of the airstrikes. As a matter of fact, they have reduced the losses of both planes and pilots. The losses of planes, for example, are rather significantly lower than we had previously estimated.

Now a word on the pacification program. You are all aware that within the past few weeks there has been a reorganization of the American effort in the pacification, an integration of the civilian and military staffs.

The responsibility for pacification has been assigned to General Westmoreland, whose deputy, Mr. Robert Komer, has been placed in direct charge of it. I was very pleased with what I saw.

The frictions that I had read about in the paper perhaps existed at one time but certainly have been dampened down, if not completely eliminated. Both civilian and military officers that I have visited at the sector level, the provinces, and the subsector levels of the villages and hamlets, were working effectively together and appeared to have benefitted from this integration and reorganization of the pacification efforts.

However, having said that, I should state to you that to be candid I must report the progress of pacification has been very slow. I think that the momentum will increase as the new organization gains in experience, but what we are really trying to do here is engage in nation-building. It is an extraordinary complex process. I would anticipate progress in what is really a very significant field would continue to be slow.

I am sure that the first question you would ask me, if I didn't anticipate it, would be about additional military personnel; so I will address myself to that. I think some more U.S. military personnel will be required. I am not sure how many. I am certain of one thing: that we must use more effectively the personnel that are presently there.

When I say that, I am speaking of all free-world personnel. As you know, the Vietnamese, the Koreans, the Australians, the New Zealanders, the Filipinos, as well as we, have all

80

contributed forces to the support of the operations in Viet-Nam. There has been a very rapid buildup of those forces. We now have in uniform of the free-world forces over 1,300,000 men. As you might expect in any organization that has expanded so fast as this one has, there are bound to be areas of waste and inefficiency that can be corrected and eliminated -- that must be corrected when we are considering additional troop requirements.

Chapter Eight

The Tet Offensive

Dissent over America's policies in Vietnam grew rapidly in the years 1965 to 1967 as the war effort was dramatically escalated. Disillusionment within the administration grew as well. Some, like Defense Secretary Robert McNamara, (the man who was once the architect of escalation), spoke for a lowering of objectives in Vietnam. In the fall of 1967, he resigned and was replaced by Clark Clifford.

In Vietnam, Thieu had strengthened his position by being elected President of the Republic of Vietnam after a power struggle with Ky. The ticket of Thieu and Ky won with only 35% of the vote in an election that featured eleven different slates of candidates. This was hardly the election mandate the U.S. would have liked.

Again, the U.S. had supported the leader it thought was the best bet to gather the support of the Vietnamese people. Again, this leader failed to provide the kind of leadership necessary to America's political aims.

Despite cautious optimism from the military, the war was at a virtual stalemate. The only U.S. tactic that appeared to be working well was the bombing of the North. Intensive bombings had begun to take a serious toll on the North, plunging its already weak economy into desperate measures. Millions of peasants had fled the cities. As a result, manufacturing was severely hurt. The rural population, already stressed with millions of acres of destroyed farmland, began to suffer from malnutrition. Still, North Vietnam was far from defeated as aid from Communist China and the Soviets increased each year. New, more advanced weapons like surface to air missiles and more powerful artillery made the PAVN an even more potent fighting force. In 1967, the Communist military leaders began to plan an offensive that they hoped would break the stalemate and convince the U.S. that only one viable option remained - withdrawal. This action came to be called the Tet Offensive, so named for the Vietnamese New Year, the time during which the offensive was launched.

Communist forces, including regular army units (PAVN), and NLF battalions, launched coordinated attacks against major cities throughout the South on January 31, 1968. A diversionary assault on the Marine camp at Khe Sanh helped provide an element of surprise to the attacks. The magnitude of the fighting was chilling. Simultaneous attacks by the NLF and PAVN forces were launched against thirty-six of the forty-four provincial capitals and five of the six major cities. The U.S. embassy, the U.S. airbase, and the Presidential Palace in Saigon were all attacked. Certainly, the American military that had depicted the tide of the war as turning, did not expect battles of this magnitude. Nonetheless, statistics show us that Tet was a major military defeat for the North. More than 40,000 communist soldiers were killed and most of the military gains made in the first few days, were quickly lost in subsequent battles. The notable exception to this was Hue, a key city in the north of South Vietnam that was taken and held for weeks by the NVA. American and South Vietnamese losses were a fraction of the communist losses. The NLF would never recover from the defeat. Yet Tet marks *the* turning point in America's involvement in Vietnam. After Tet, LBJ began to move toward negotiation. Public support for the war decreased rapidly. The anti-war movement gained increased credibility and the military suffered a credibility gap. How could a military defeat for the North turn into their biggest political victory of the war?

To examine this question, we must first look at the goals of the North in planning this offensive. Ideally, the North saw a massive, coordinated attack across South Vietnam as leading to a general uprising that would remove President Thieu. A new regime would then form that would include communists in a coalition government. If the general uprising failed to arise, the sheer size of the attack would, it was hoped, convince the U.S. of the resolve and ability of the North to fight a prolonged war. It would also help convince the American public, whose support was already beginning to wane, that this was an unwinnable war. Faced with loss of support at home, a still powerful enemy in Vietnam, and a weak government in the South, the U.S. would be faced with no option but withdrawal. The ideal situation the communists hoped for did not occur. There was no popular uprising. But the secondary goal of trying to shape U.S. policy in Vietnam was achieved.

Tet pointed out the failures of U.S. policy in Vietnam. Without the support of the South Vietnamese people, the coordinated and massive attacks could never have occurred. Tet shook the faith of Americans and the South Vietnamese as it proved that no place in Vietnam, not even the American Embassy, was safe. Communists were viewed by the South Vietnamese as folk heroes standing up to the Americans who were just another colonial power like France. The credibility lost by the American military and LBJ and his advisers was won by the communists. Anti-war spokespersons in America and Vietnam gained new popularity. Even some of LBJ's advisers began to search for a way out of the quagmire of Vietnam. No other event in the war showed so clearly the bankruptcy of U.S. policy.

Nowhere was that bankruptcy as clear as it was in the American military command. Westmoreland had said in 1967 that there was "light at the end of the tunnel", meaning he foresaw an end to the war in the near future and a U.S. victory. The massive, well-coordinated attack in the Tet offensive seriously hurt Westmoreland's credibility.

During the TET offensive NLF soldiers had managed to invade the American compound in Saigon before being shot and killed. When Westmoreland held a televised press conference in the compound it brought into the living rooms of America the vivid image of Westmoreland surrounded by the dead bodies of NLF soldiers. American audiences could no longer ignore the irony in Westmoreland's claims of success.

The general's call for an additional 200,000 troops was

86

greeted with skepticism by Americans who were disenchanted with an expensive war half a world away. Congress and the President began to feel increasing pressure at home as race riots plagued the streets and Dr. Martin Luther King and presidential candidate Robert Kennedy were both assassinated. The domestic agenda grew in importance and the anti-war movement grew in power. Both Kennedy and King, before their deaths, had challenged LBJ's position on Vietnam. A new, pro-peace Democratic candidate for the presidency, Eugene McCarthy, was gaining in popularity. America was becoming increasingly divided over issues of race, civil rights, dissent, and the war.

In March of 1968, LBJ called together his "Wise Men," who were a group of old and new foreign policy advisers. Their job was to evaluate the military's request for 200,000 additional troops. In a shocking reversal of their stance of 1965, most of these advisers now warned the president that the war was unwinnable and de-escalation was the best policy. It was as a result of this meeting that LBJ made the following speech. It was a notable speech for two reasons. First, he renews a call for negotiations with the North and announces a partial bombing halt, and second, he makes the most startling announcement of his Presidency, that he will not run for a second full term in 1968. Consider these questions as you study Johnson's speech.

Checkpoint

1. What incentive does LBJ offer to try to get the North to negotiate? What effect do you think this had on his critics at home?

2. What is the economic message he is trying to convey to Congress and to the American people?

3. Publicly, what does LBJ give as his reason for not running for re-election in 1968? Speculate on his private reasons for not seeking re-election.

4. What effect does a President's success or failure in war time have on his political future? List Presidents who have been re-elected, at least partially, on the basis of military accomplishments.

Lyndon B. Johnson, Televised Public Address, March 31, 1968.

Good evening my fellow Americans. Tonight I want to speak to you of peace in Viet-Nam and Southeast Asia.

No other question so preoccupies our people. No other dream so absorbs the 250 million human beings who live in that part of the world. No other goal motivates American policy in Southeast Asia.

For years, representatives of our Government and others have traveled the world seeking to find a basis for peace talks.

Since last September, they have carried the offer that I made public in San Antonio.

That offer was this: that the United States would stop its

bombardment of North Viet-Nam when that would lead promptly to productive discussions -- and that we would assume that North Viet-Nam would not take military advantage of our restraint.

Hanoi denounced this offer, both privately and publicly. Even while the search for peace was going on, North Viet-Nam rushed their preparations for a savage assault on the people, the Government, and the allies of South Viet-Nam.

Their attack -- during the Tet holidays -- failed to achieve its principal objectives.

It did not collapse the elected government of South Viet-Nam or shatter its army, as the Communists had hoped.

It did not produce a "general uprising" among the people of the cities, as they had predicted.

The Communists were unable to maintain control of any of the more than 30 cities they had attacked. And they took very heavy casualties.

But they did not compel the South Vietnamese and their allies to move certain forces from the countryside into the cities. They caused widespread disruption and suffering. Their attacks, and the battles that followed, made refugees of half a million human beings.

The Communists may renew their attack any day. They are, it appears, trying to make 1968 the year of decision in South Viet-Nam -- the year that brings, if not final victory or defeat, at least a turning point in the struggle.

This much is clear: If they do mount another round of heavy attacks, they will not succeed in destroying the fighting power of South Viet-Nam and its allies.

But tragically, this is also clear: Many men -- on both sides of the struggle -- will be lost. A nation that has already suffered 20 years of warfare will suffer once again. Armies on both sides will take new casualties. And the war will go on.

There is no need for this to be so.

There is no need to delay the talks that could bring an end to this long and this bloody war.

Tonight I renew the offer I made last August -- to stop the bombardment of North Viet-Nam. We ask that talks begin promptly, that they be serious talks on the substance of peace. We assume that during those talks Hanoi will not take advantage of our restraint.

We are prepared to move immediately toward peace through negotiations. So tonight, in the hope that this action will lead to early talks, I am taking the first step to de-escalate the conflict. We are reducing -- substantially reducing -- the present level of hostilities. And we are doing so unilaterally and at once.

Tonight I have ordered our aircraft and our naval vessels to make no attacks on North Viet-Nam, except in the area north of the demilitarized zone where the continuing enemy buildup directly threatens Allied forward positions and where the movements of their troops and supplies are clearly related to that threat.

The area in which we are stopping our attacks includes almost 90 percent of North Viet-Nam's population and most of its territory. Thus there will be no attacks around the principal populated areas or in the food-producing areas of North Viet-Nam.

Even this very limited bombing of the North could come to an early end if our restraint is matched by restraint in Hanoi. But I cannot in good conscience stop all bombing so long as to do so would immediately and directly endanger the lives of our men and our allies. Whether a complete bombing halt becomes possible in the future will be determined by events.

Our purpose in this action is to bring about a reduction in the level of violence that now exists.

It is to save the lives of brave men and to save the lives of innocent women and children. It is to permit the contending forces to move closer to a political settlement.

And tonight I call upon the United Kingdom and I call upon the Soviet Union, as co-chairmen of the Geneva conferences and as permanent members of the United Nations Security Council, to do all they can to move from the unilateral act of de-escalation that I have just announced toward genuine peace in Southeast Asia.

Now, as in the past, the United States is ready to send its representatives to any forum, at any time, to discuss the means of bringing this ugly war to an end.

I am designating one of our most distinguished Americans, Ambassador Averell Harriman, as my personal representative

90

for such talks. In addition, I have asked Ambassador Llewellyn Thompson, who returned from Moscow for consultation, to be available to join Ambassador Harriman at Geneva or any other suitable place just as soon as Hanoi agrees to a conference.

I call upon President Ho Chi Minh to respond positively and favorably to this new step toward peace.

But if peace does not come now through negotiations, it will come when Hanoi understands that our common resolve is unshakable and our common strength is invincible.

Tonight, we and the other allied nations are contributing 600,000 fighting men to assist 700,000 South Vietnamese troops in defending their little country.

Our presence there has always rested on this basic belief: The main burden of preserving their freedom must be carried out by them -- by the South Vietnamese themselves.

We and our allies can only help to provide a shield behind which the people of South Viet-nam can survive and can grow and develop. On their efforts -- on their determinations and resourcefulness -- the outcome will ultimately depend....

The actions that we have taken since the beginning of the year to re-equip the South Vietnamese forces; to meet our responsibilities in Korea, as well as our responsibilities in Viet-Nam; to meet the price increases and the cost of activating and deploying Reserve forces; to replace helicopters and provide the other military supplies we need -- all of these actions are going to require additional expenditures.

The tentative estimate of those expenditures is $2.5 billion in this fiscal year and $2.6 billion in the next fiscal year.

These projected increases in expenditures for our national security will bring into sharper focus the Nation's need for immediate action, action to protect the prosperity of the American people and to protect the strength and the stability of our American dollar.

On many occasions I have pointed out that without a tax bill or decreased expenditures next year's deficit would again be around $20 billion. I have emphasized the need to set strict priorities in our spending. I have stressed that failure to act -- and to act promptly and decisively -- would raise very strong doubts throughout the world about America's willingness to keep its financial house in order.

Yet Congress has not acted. And tonight we face the sharpest financial threat of the post-war era -- a threat to the dollar's rate as the keystone of international trade and finance in the world....

One day, my fellow citizens, there will be peace in Southeast Asia.

It will come because the people of Southeast Asia want it -- those whose armies are at war tonight and those who, though threatened, have thus far been spared.

Peace will come because Asians were willing to work for it -- and to sacrifice for it -- and to die by the thousands for it.

But let it never be forgotten: Peace will also come because America sent her sons to help secure it.

It has not been easy -- far from it. During the past 4 1\2 years, it has been my fate and my responsibility to be Commander in Chief. I lived daily and nightly with the cost of this war. I know the pain that it has inflicted. I know perhaps better than anyone the misgivings that it has aroused.

Throughout this entire long period, I have been sustained by a single principle: that what we are doing now in Viet-Nam is vital not only to the security of Southeast Asia, but it is vital to the security of every American.

Surely we have treaties which we must respect. Surely we have commitments that we are going to keep. Resolutions of the Congress testify to the need to resist aggression in the world and in Southeast Asia.

But the heart of our involvement in South Viet-Nam -- under three different Presidents, three separate administrations -- has always been America's own security.

And the larger purpose of our involvement has always been to help the nations of Southeast Asia become independent and stand alone, self-sustaining as members of the great world community -- at peace with themselves and at peace with all others.

With such an Asia, our country -- and the world -- will be far more secure than it is tonight.

I believe that a peaceful Asia is far nearer to reality because of what America has done in Viet-Nam. I believe that the men who endure the dangers of battle -- fighting there for us tonight -- are helping the entire world avoid far greater conflicts, far wider wars, far more destruction, than this one. The peace that will bring them home some day will come. Tonight I have offered the first in what I hope will be a series of mutual moves toward peace.

I pray that it will not be rejected by the leaders of North Viet-Nam. I pray that they will accept it as a means by which the sacrifices of their own people may be ended. And I ask your help and your support, my fellow citizens, for this effort to reach across the battlefield toward an early peace....

Throughout my entire public career I have followed the personal philosophy that I am a free man, an American, a public servant, and a member of my party, in that order always and only.

For 37 years in the service of our nation, first as a Congressman, as a Senator and as Vice President and now as your President, I have put the unity of the people first. I have put it ahead of any divisive partisanship.

And in these times as in times before, it is true that a house divided against itself by the spirit of faction, of party, or region, of religion, of race, is a house that cannot stand.

There is a division in the American house now. There is divisiveness among us all tonight. And holding the trust that is mine, as President of all people, I cannot disregard the peril to the progress of the American people and the hope and the prospect for peace for all peoples.

So I would ask all Americans, whatever their personal interests or concern, to guard against divisiveness and all its ugly consequences.

Fifty-two months and ten days ago, in a moment of tragedy and trauma, the duties of this Office fell upon me. I asked then for your help and for God's, that we might continue America on its course, binding up our wounds, healing our history, moving forward in new unity, to clear the American agenda and to keep the American commitment for all of our people.

United we have kept that commitment. United we have enlarged that commitment.

Through all time to come, I think America will be a stronger nation, a more just society, and a land of greater opportunity and fulfillment because of what we have done together in these years of unparalled achievement.

Our reward will come in the life of freedom, peace, and hope that our children will enjoy through ages ahead.

What we won when all of our people united just must not now be lost in suspicion, distrust, selfishness, and politics among any of our people.

Believing this as I do, I have concluded that I should not permit the Presidency to become involved in the partisan divisions that are developing in this political year.

With America's sons in the fields far away, with America's future under challenge right here at home, with our hopes and the world's hopes for peace in the balance every day, I do not believe that I should devote an hour or a day of my time to any personal partisan causes or to any duties other than the awesome duties of this Office -- the Presidency of your country.

Accordingly, I shall not seek, and I will not accept, the nomination of my party for another term as your President.

But let men everywhere know, however, that a strong, a confident, and a vigilant America stands ready tonight to seek an honorable peace -- and stands ready tonight to defend an honored cause -- whatever the price, whatever the burden, whatever the sacrifices that duty may require.

Thank you for listening.

Good night and God bless all of you.

Chapter Nine

The Movement

Public policies on Vietnam, as you have read, were shaped by three forces: international constraints, developments within Vietnam, and developments within the U.S. This chapter deals with the latter. Little has been said in this book about the anti-war movement in the U.S. The movement brings up some important questions about the war and about the American public. Did the anti-war movement lengthen or shorten the war? Were protesters patriots or traitors? What are the legitimate limits of dissent in wartime? What have been some of the lasting effects of the movement on the American psyche?

To answer these questions, we must first look at the background of the anti-war movement and some of the key players. The anti-war movement was a product of two protest movements of the fifties, the Ban the Bomb, or anti-nuclear movement, and the civil rights movement. Both used confrontational, non-violent civil disobedience to try to influence public policy. Members of these groups included religionists like the Quakers and Methodists. Other members were scientists opposed to the testing and stockpiling of nuclear weapons. Still others were liberal reformers who wished to improve the civil rights of minorities and reduce the threat of nuclear extermination. Lastly, there was a small but vocal group of radical pacifists who challenged the basic assumptions of our American system. They sought nothing less than the total restructuring of American society. Some of these were communists or socialists. Some were democrats who wished to see a more democratic (fair and just) society. By the late 1950's, these groups were advocating an end to the testing of nuclear weapons and an end to discrimination against minorities. Student organizations on college campuses adopted both causes and united the two issues.

Most famous of these student organizations in the early sixties was the SDS (Students for a Democratic Society). The group evolved from the radical pacifist branch of the anti-nuclear movement. Their Port Huron Statement, issued in 1962, was a challenge to basic assumptions that guided American foreign policy. Tom Hayden, author of the manifesto (statement of aims), questioned basic ideas such as containment, nuclear deterrence, and the democratic system in the U.S. The SDS grew in membership as students at college campuses across the nation joined the peace movement in the early sixties. At this time, the peace movement consisted of those opposed to nuclear weapons testing and in favor of civil rights. Soon, that movement would turn from a peace movement to an anti-war movement as the U.S. escalated intervention in Vietnam.

The events of 1964 to 1965 brought about this change. The Gulf of Tonkin Resolution and the decisions to commit ground troops and begin Operation Rolling Thunder made the war more visible. An opinion poll in 1964 indicated that one in every four Americans was unaware of a war in Southeast Asia. Two-thirds paid little or no attention to news coming from the area. Those figures changed dramatically as escalation began.

America began to polarize into three groups. The first group were the hawks; usually conservative and firmly committed to a military victory in Vietnam. They were frustrated by the limited war being fought in Indochina. Wartime policy, prior to the Korean War, called for total victory, unconditional surrender, and sacrifice and commitment at home. Hawks had difficulty accepting the international constraints that limited the effectiveness of American firepower. Some proposed using nuclear weapons to, as Air Force General Curtis LeMay said, "Bomb them back to the Stone Age." On the left were the doves. Some favored immediate withdrawal from Vietnam. Others wished to see a gradual withdrawal and total responsibility for the war placed on the Vietnamese. The doves questioned basic assumptions of American foreign policy like containment, the monolithic structure of communism, and the domino theory. In between these two groups was the great majority of people in the United States. In 1964 they knew and cared little about American intervention in Vietnam. It became the goal of the anti-war movement to "raise the consciousness" of Americans. In 1965, the SDS released the statement below. As you read it, try to answer these questions:

Checkpoint

1. Analyze the statement in the second paragraph "that it is fought alongside a regime with no claim to represent its people." Do you agree or disagree with this statement? Why?

2. What alternatives to military service does the SDS propose? Why did it try to center on domestic problems in the U.S.? Each year, the U.S. spends billions of dollars giving economic aid to Third World countries while domestic issues of drug abuse, crime, homelessness, etc. go unanswered. How do you feel about this? Why do you think the U.S. provides aid to these countries?

3. Some countries such as Israel have compulsory military service. Congress has proposed, but not passed, legislation that would require Americans to serve in the military, the Peace Corps, or a domestic organization like VISTA (Volunteers in Service to America). How would you feel about being compelled to perform such a duty? If given a choice between the military and an organization like VISTA, which would you choose?

4. Conscientious objectors cannot be forced to serve in the military if they have strong moral or religious objections to war. In the last paragraph, the SDS advises everyone of draft age to register as a conscientious objector. In WWI people who gave this advice were jailed. Research the case *Schenck v. U.S.* What was the reason given for arresting Schenck? No one in the Vietnam War era was arrested and tried on the same grounds. Why not? Does public policy on free speech change with the times? What factors shape this change? Other cases you may want to research include *Dennis v. U.S.* and *Yates v. U.S.*

Students for a Democratic Society, Press Release, October, 1965.

Students for a Democratic Society wishes to reiterate emphatically its intention to pursue its opposition to the war in Vietnam, undeterred by the diversionary tactics of the administration.

We feel that the war is immoral at its root, that it is fought alongside a regime with no claim to represent its people, and that *it is foreclosing the hope of making America a decent and truly democratic society.*

The commitment of SDS, and of the whole generation we represent, is clear: we are anxious to build villages; we refuse to burn them. We are anxious to help and to change our country; we refuse to destroy someone else's country. We are anxious to advance the cause of democracy; we do not believe that cause can be advanced by torture and terror.

We are fully prepared to volunteer for service to our country and to democracy. We volunteer to go into Watts to work with the people of Watts to rebuild that neighborhood to be the kind of place that the people of Watts want it to be -- and when we say "rebuild,", we mean   socially as well as physically. We volunteer to help the Peace Corps learn, as we have been learning in the slums and in Mississippi, how to energize the hungry and desperate and defeated of the world to make big decisions. We volunteer to serve in hospitals and schools in the slums, in the Job Corps and VISTA, in the new Teachers Corps -- and to do so in such a way as to strengthen democracy at its grass-roots. And in order to make our volunteering possible, we propose to the President that all those Americans who seek so vigorously to build instead of burn be given their chance to do so. We propose that he test the young people of America: if they had a free choice, would they want to burn and torture in Vietnam or to build a democracy at home and overseas? There is only one way to make the choice real: let us see what happens if service to democracy is made grounds for exemption to the military draft. I predict that almost every member of my generation would choose to build, not to burn; to teach, not to torture; to help, not to kill. And I am sure that the overwhelming majority of our brothers and cousins in the

army in Vietnam, would make the same choice if they could --
to serve and build, not kill and destroy....

Until the President agrees to our proposal, we have only one
choice: we do in conscience object, utterly and wholeheartedly,
to this war; and we will encourage every member of our
generation to object, and to file his objection through the Form
150 provided by the law for conscientious objection.

Chapter Ten

The Anti-War Movement Gains Credibility

The most vocal critics of the war in 1965 were to be found on college campuses across the nation. These included UCLA at Berkeley, the University of Wisconsin, Columbia University, and scores of others. But protesters in 1965 were still a small minority. Polls indicated that college students supported the war as much or more than their parents. It was easy to provide such support when the draft system granted exemptions to those in college. This system was discriminatory as it rejected those who had no skills or were attending college.

By 1967, the draft exemption ended as it became clear that vast new reserves of troops would be necessary to carry out the war effort. Selective Service reformed the system and ended the college exemption. Nothing galvanized opposition to the war among the young like the military draft. It became the focal point of the anti-war movement on college campuses. Some protesters chose to burn their draft cards or their draft notices in public demonstrations. Thousands resisted the draft by fleeing to

Canada or Europe. In 1968 alone, over 3300 men were prosecuted for resisting the draft as conscientious objectors. The reasons for resisting the draft were many. Some felt all war to be immoral. Others felt this particular war to be immoral and refused to participate. (In a case devised to test this premise, *U.S. v. Seeger*, the Supreme Court declined conscientious objector status on the basis of objections to a *particular* war.) Other draft age young men simply refused to serve on the basis of their doubts about the value or intent of this war. To them, the objectives seemed unclear and the cause questionable. These resisters were simply unwilling to sacrifice the promise of their future for a cause in which they did not believe. Some called these young men traitors for resisting their country's call to arms. Some called them patriots for their willingness to resist the system and an unjust war. Resisters who fled could not return for fear of arrest and imprisonment until a draft amnesty was put into effect in the 1970's. Often, those who stayed and resisted were arrested and imprisoned, while others moved around the country under false names trying to avoid the FBI.

The anti-war movement was not just a campus phenomenon. In fact, the student protests drew an increasing amount of media attention which fueled debate at most levels of the public and the government. Those who did directly affect LBJ and Nixon were the intellectuals. They included writers for prominent newspapers like *The New York Times* and *The Washington Post* and journals of opinion such as *The New Republic*. College professors also led the intellectual opposition. Many participated in "teach-ins" designed to educate the public on the issues of the war. Teachers joined with students in the increasingly frequent demonstrations, carrying placards with anti-war messages and chanting (of the draft) "Hell No We Won't Go!" or "Hey, Hey LBJ, How Many Kids Did You Kill Today?" The intellectual opposition to the war played a vital part in the movement as it clearly stated the goals of the movement and pointed out the inconsistencies in U.S. foreign policy. In short, the intellectuals in the movement gave it a voice that was heard beyond the reaches of the campus.

Intellectuals challenged the basic assumptions that were guiding U.S. policy on the war. One of the most important of the intellectual critics of the war by 1966 was George F. Kennan. Kennan was the scholar and diplomat who authored the policy of containment in the late 1940's. He echoed Ball's interpretation that the U.S. should take its lumps now and avoid a protracted war with exorbitant costs.

LBJ tried to dismiss the intellectuals who challenged him but he did track their writings in *The Post* and *The Times*. Among the most influential and widely read of these intellectuals was Walter Lippmann. Lippmann detested the bombing of Vietnam claiming that such tactics deprived the U.S. of any moral justification for the war. Lippmann and other intellectuals were also angered by the duplicity of the Johnson administration. This duplicity included lying to the public and to Congress.

Perhaps swayed by the passion and growth of the anti-war movement, some politicians like Senators Frank Church and J. William Fulbright began to openly challenge LBJ's ideas on Vietnam. Fulbright had been instrumental in moving the Gulf of Tonkin Resolution through the Senate in 1964. His support came after a meeting with

LBJ in which LBJ promised to use the resolution for retaliatory purposes only. Fulbright felt betrayed and used by LBJ when the Gulf Resolution was used by the President to widen the war in 1965 and 1966. He used his power as head of the Senate Foreign Relations Committee to hold hearings in 1966 on the Vietnam War. He called in various presidential advisers to defend the nation's role in Vietnam. This infuriated LBJ and convinced him to avoid seeking advice from this important committee. Thus, the Senate Foreign Relations committee, which should have been providing valuable input, was effectively excluded by the executive from the policy making process.

Intellectuals performed invaluable services to the movement. They legitimized dissent by presenting clear arguments against American intervention in Vietnam. They presented those arguments in ways that made it possible for others to frame their own opinions on the war. They pointed out the inconsistencies of U.S. policy and the faulty assumptions upon which policy was based. They stressed the immorality of the war and kept this issue in the public eye. They brought the universities to the forefront of the movement and encouraged student activism. In short, intellectuals kept the heat on the administrations of Johnson and later Nixon to bring the war to a close. While students and demonstrations attracted the media, and brought pressure to bear on players thus far excluded from policy-making, anti-war intellectuals successfully gained the attention of the president and his advisers, who were actually making the war policies.

Public Policy Analysis - Monitoring

The first step in analyzing a public policy issue is to monitor the conditions that are present (see Chapter 1). One way to do this is to monitor public opinion on the issue. The Gallup and Harris organizations, professional poll-taking companies, conducted many opinion polls on the war during the sixties. The graph that follows charts Americans' responses over time to a basic question about the war. The question asked was "In view of the developments since we entered the fighting in Vietnam, do you think the U.S. made a mistake sending troops to fight in Vietnam?" Based on the graph, and your knowledge of the events of the war through 1968, try to answer the following questions.

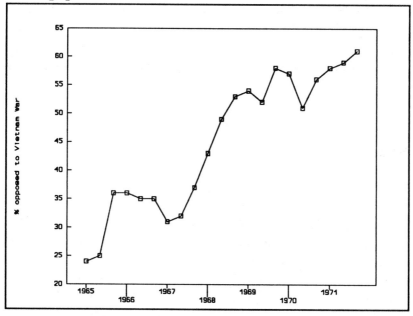

Opposition to U.S. troop involvement in Vietnam, 1965-1971. From *The Gallup Opinion Index,* no. 73 (July 1971), p.3.

1. What was the initial reaction on the part of the public to the commitment of ground forces in 1965? What explains this?

2. In 1967 public opinion in opposition to the war begins to fall. What explains this?

3. What pivotal event in 1968 causes a sharp increase in public opposition?

4. Overall, the graph shows a general increase in public opposition to the war over the years 1966-1971. What were the factors that led to this increase? What players were shaping public opinion in these years?

Shaping Public Policy and Opinion

Fire became a symbol for the war and the anti-war movement. In Vietnam, napalm was used to destroy North Vietnamese enclaves but many civilians died in its wake. In 1963, a Buddhist monk, Thich Quang Duc, set himself afire in Saigon protesting the policies of Diem. Americans burned their draft cards. And in November of 1965, a Quaker, Norman Morrison, doused himself and his year and a half old infant with kerosene and set himself and his child afire on the steps of the Pentagon. The child was

106

saved, Morrison died. Not all demonstrations were as dramatic and tragic as this one. But as the casualties mounted, so did the actions of the movement.

The anti-war movement was never a single, cohesive organization with a powerful leader. There was no card that identified one as a member of the movement -- you were just part of it if you opposed the war. As LBJ escalated the ground and air war in Vietnam, anti-war organizations turned to more confrontational tactics designed to gain publicity and educate the public on the actions of their government in Southeast Asia.

These actions included sit-ins in college administration buildings. Students would occupy offices until college administration officials agreed to their demands. Such demands included the removal of ROTC (Reserve Officer Training Corps) programs. Others demanded that universities refuse to accept support from companies that made war-related products. One company that was frequently targeted was Dow Chemical. Dow was infamous for being involved in the manufacture of napalm. Any company that was tied into the military industrial complex was considered fair game for these demands.

The Vietnam War has been called the "Living Room War" since nightly news broadcasts carried reports via satellite directly from the battlefield to America's televisions. One of the goals of the anti-war movement was to gain as much television exposure as possible. An effective means of doing this was the mass protest or march. Thousands of people would converge to march and listen to speeches protesting the war. The Easter Demonstration in 1965 brought together 20,000 demonstrators in Washington D.C. A demonstration in New York City in 1967 brought together tens of thousands.

Students protesting the war disrupted the Democratic National Convention in 1968. As demonstrations grew in intensity and size, so did the police response. Demonstrators attempting to gain a strategic area tried to break through police lines causing escalation from shoving to stone and bottle-throwing to beatings and even bullets. The actions of the Chicago police in beating protesters at the convention hurt the chances of election for the Democratic candidate, Hubert Humphrey. Some within the movement, angered by what they saw as police brutality, took to violence themselves thereby betraying the principles of non-violence on which the movement was founded. One such group, a splinter faction of the SDS called the Weathermen, resorted to the bombing of military facilities. In one such incident in 1970, a graduate student at the University of Wisconsin was killed by a bomb placed at a military research facility on the campus. These incidents, though few in number, severely hurt the credibility of the movement.

In addition to this, the movement was becoming increasingly identified with the counter-culture in America. This new culture rejected the materialism of its elders and called upon the youth of America to "Tune in, turn on, and drop out." Based as it was on drug use, rock music, and free sex, the counter-culture alienated large groups of older Americans who had begun to question the war. Many of these began to ask of the protesters, "What is your goal, to end the war or to change America?" Many within the movement, frustrated with the continued escalation of the

108

war, began to feel that the one could not be obtained without the other. Those who could not identify with the movement but were opposed to the war looked for a reasonable and honorable way out of the quagmire of Vietnam. Richard Nixon in 1968 claimed to have the answer in a secret plan to end the war. Americans voted him into office in the hope that he could, as he promised, produce peace with honor.

Checkpoint

1. What actions did the movement take that alienated people who favored an end to U.S. commitment in Vietnam? What actions attracted people to the cause?

2. Is it reasonable to assume that the extensive television coverage of the Vietnam war set a precedent for all following conflicts to be brought into the living rooms of America?

3. During World War II and prior wars, the American people obtained information primarily through the newspapers. Do you think that "living room" coverage of a war would result in a different public opinion than would newspaper coverage? Why?

Chapter Eleven

After Tet

Decisive events in 1968 shaped America's public policy in Vietnam for the remainder of the war. Johnson did not run for re-election, pledging to devote his time to seeking a negotiated settlement of the war. Richard Nixon entered the Oval Office with a vague promise of a quick end to the war and a pledge not to widen the war into neighboring Cambodia. The Tet Offensive helped turn American public opinion against the war. Violence in the streets at home and the tragic assassinations of Martin Luther King and Robert Kennedy convinced many people that the U.S. needed to concentrate on domestic problems.

As public support continued to wane and the anti-war movement gained in popularity, Nixon and his key foreign policy adviser, Henry Kissinger, began to search for a way out of the war. The challenge lay in finding a way to maintain credibility while removing U.S. forces from the battlefield. Later, Nixon would clarify these restraints with the simple but powerful phrase, "peace with honor." The decision-making process continued to be confined to the executive branch. As the next fateful decision neared, only the President and his closest adviser would be involved.

The events of 1968 and the decline in public support for the war convinced Nixon and Kissinger that the war was unwinnable given the constraints they faced. They formulated a policy that was designed to attain three objectives. The first objective was to open negotiations with the North Vietnamese. President Nixon hoped to boost South Vietnamese control over the rural areas and thus be able to negotiate from a position of strength. The second goal was to appease some of the anti-war critics by beginning to withdraw U.S. forces. To this end, in June of 1969, Nixon announced the withdrawal of 25,000 U.S. troops. Thirdly, the President hoped to quicken the pace of negotiations by improving the South Vietnamese Army and shutting off the North's supply routes that ran through Laos and Cambodia. This was to be accomplished through the bombing of communist enclaves in Cambodia and a gradual turning over of the war to the South Vietnamese military.

This policy of gradual withdrawal and delegation of responsibility for the completion of the war to the South Vietnamese was called *Vietnamization.* By the summer of 1969, Nixon and his advisers had abandoned plans of winning the war in Vietnam. In its place was a plan that called for a diminishing U.S. military presence, increased aid to the South Vietnamese, and a negotiated settlement that would preserve the credibility of the U.S. Secret talks between U.S. and North Vietnamese negotiators began in Paris without the participation of South Vietnam. Still, it would be more than three years before the war would actually end. Many people have asked since then, if the

U.S. was planning on leaving anyway, why did it take three years to accomplish the withdrawal?

Richard Nixon suffered through a very close election against Hubert Humphrey in 1968. His paranoid mentality saw a potential Democratic challenger for 1972 under every rock. The slow process of Vietnamization would insure that he would not be seen as the President who lost Vietnam, at least not before the 1972 election. Vietnamization gave the appearance of returning the responsibility of the war to the Vietnamese. In truth, Vietnamization was a delaying tactic to preserve Nixon's anti-communist reputation through 1972. After that time, Vietnam could, and would be forsaken without political fallout. The fateful decision to turn the war over to the Vietnamese was once again made without public debate or Congressional approval. But where JFK and LBJ had consulted a fairly large group of advisers, Nixon restricted these decisions to Kissinger and himself. The already limited debate on the war had become smaller and smaller.

Another fateful decision involved expanding the war into Cambodia. Nixon had promised in his election campaign in 1968 to avoid widening the war. Communists were using neutral Cambodia as a staging area for operations in South Vietnam. Nixon ordered bombing and troop incursions to attack these enclaves. This "secret war" in Cambodia, and the equally secret bombing of neighboring Laos, once revealed, enraged Congress and the American public. These actions would finally lead Congress to begin restricting the powers of the President. The War Powers Act of 1973 was a direct result of the abuse of presidential power and the improper ways in which public policy was being formulated.

113

Vietnamization provided the ARVN with better arms and supplies. Land and election reforms in the countryside helped build something of a political base for President Thieu. Pacification programs, designed to use ARVN forces to maintain areas won by allied forces, were better able to hold territory as communist forces had withdrawn and regrouped from some areas after the defeat of Tet.

In the speech that follows, President Nixon describes the Nixon Doctrine and the basic plan for Vietnamization. As you read the text, try to answer the following questions.

Checkpoint

1. Why does Nixon renounce the "popular and easy course" of immediate withdrawal?

2. Nixon argues that withdrawal would lead to more war, not peace. Explain this argument. Do you support this point of view? Why or why not? Even though he does not name it, what historical analogy is he using to support his arguments?

3. How did the Nixon Doctrine differ from LBJ's ideas on how to conduct the war?

4. Nixon was hoping for a favorable response from the North Vietnamese after this speech. But the North did not soften its stance on reuniting Vietnam and the war dragged on. How could Nixon have increased the chances for peace at this time? What proposals could he have made?

5. Finally, in the last three paragraphs, Nixon mentions the most compelling reason for continuing the war. What was that reason?

Richard M. Nixon, Televised Public Address, November 24, 1969.

Good evening, my fellow Americans: Tonight I want to talk to you on a subject of deep concern to all Americans and to many people in all parts of the world -- the war in Viet-Nam.

I believe that one of the reasons for the deep division about Viet-Nam is that many Americans have lost confidence in what their Government has told them about our policy. The

American people cannot and should not be asked to support a policy which involves the overriding issues of war and peace unless they know the truth about that policy.

Tonight, therefore, I would like to answer some of the questions that I know are on the minds of many of you listening to me.

How and why did America get involved in Viet-Nam in the first place?

How has this administration changed the policy of the previous administration?

What has really happened in the negotiations in Paris and on the battlefront in Viet-Nam?

What choices do we have if we are to end the war?

What are the prospects for peace?

Let me begin by describing the situation I found when I was inaugurated on January 20.

. The war had been going on for 4 years.

. 31,000 Americans had been killed in action.

. The training program for the South Vietnamese was behind schedule.

. 540,000 Americans were in Viet-Nam, with no plans to reduce the number.

. No progress had been made at the negotiations in Paris and the United States had not put forth a comprehensive peace proposal.

. The war was causing deep division at home and criticism from many of our friends, as well as our enemies, abroad.

In view of these circumstances there were some who urged that I end the war at once by ordering the immediate withdrawal of all American forces.

From a political standpoint this would have been a popular and easy course to follow. After all, we became involved in the war while my predecessor was in office. I could blame the defeat which would be the result of my action on him and come out as the peacemaker. Some put it to me quite bluntly: This was the only way to avoid allowing Johnson's war to become Nixon's war.

But I had a greater obligation than to think only of the years of my administration and the next election. I had to think of the effect of my decision on the next generation and on

116

the future of peace and freedom in America and in the world.

Let us all understand that the question before us is not whether some Americans are for peace and some Americans are against peace. The question at issue is not whether Johnson's war becomes Nixon's war.

The great question is : How can we win America's peace?

Let us now turn to the fundamental issue. Why and how did the United States become involved in Viet-Nam in the first place?

Fifteen years ago North Viet-Nam, with the logistical support of Communist China and the Soviet Union, launched a campaign to impose a Communist government on South Viet-Nam by instigating and supporting a revolution.

In response to the request of the Government of South Viet-Nam, President Eisenhower sent economic aid and military equipment to assist the people of South Viet-Nam in their efforts to prevent a Communist takeover. Seven years ago President Kennedy sent 16,000 military personnel to Viet-Nam as combat advisors. Four years ago President Johnson sent American combat forces to South Viet-Nam.

Now, many believe that President Johnson's decision to send American combat forces to Viet-Nam was wrong. And many others, I among them, have been strongly critical of the way the war has been conducted.

But the question facing us today is: Now that we are in the war, what is the best way to end it?

In January I could only conclude that the precipitate withdrawal of American forces from Viet-Nam would be a disaster not only for South Viet-Nam but for the United States and for the cause of peace.

For the South Vietnamese, our precipitate withdrawal would inevitably allow the Communists to repeat the massacres which followed their takeover in the North 15 years before.

. They then murdered more than 50,000 people, and hundreds of thousands more died in slave labor camps.

. We saw a prelude of what would happen in South Viet-Nam when the Communists entered the city of Hue last year. During their brief rule there, there was a bloody reign of terror in which 3,000 civilians were clubbed, shot to

117

death, and buried in mass graves.

. With the sudden collapse of our support, these atrocities of
Hue would become the nightmare of the entire nation -- and
particularly for the million and a half Catholic refugees who
fled to South Viet-Nam when the Communists took over the
North.

For the United States, this first defeat in our nation's
history would result in a collapse of confidence in American
leadership not only in Asia but throughout the world.

Three American Presidents have recognized the great stakes
involved in Viet-Nam and understood what had to be done.

In 1963 President Kennedy, with his characteristic
eloquence and clarity, said:

>...we want to see a stable government there, carrying
>on a struggle to maintain its national independence.
>We believe strongly in that. We are not going to
>withdraw from that effort. In my opinion, for us to
>withdraw from our effort would mean a collapse not
>only of South Viet-Nam, but Southeast Asia. So we
>are going to stay there.

President Eisenhower and President Johnson expressed the
same conclusion during their terms of office.

For the future of peace, precipitate withdrawal would thus
be a disaster of immense magnitude.

. A nation cannot remain great if it betrays its allies and lets
down its friends.

. Our defeat and humiliation in South Viet-Nam without
question would promote recklessness in the councils of those
great powers who have not yet abandoned their goals of
world conquest.

. This would spark violence wherever our commitments help
maintain the peace -- in the Middle East, in Berlin,
eventually even in the Western Hemisphere.

Ultimately, this would cost more lives. It would not bring
peace; it would bring more war.

For these reasons I rejected the recommendation that I
should end the war by immediately withdrawing all our forces.
I chose instead to change American policy on both the

negotiating front and the battlefront....

It has become clear that the obstacle in negotiating an end to the war is not the President of the United States. It is not the South Vietnamese Government.

The obstacle is the other side's absolute refusal to show the least willingness to join us in seeking a just peace. It will not do so while it is convinced that all it has to do is to wait for our next concession, and our next concession after that one, until it gets everything it wants.

There can now be no longer any question that progress in negotiation depends only on Hanoi's deciding to negotiate, to negotiate seriously.

I realize that this report on our efforts on the diplomatic front is discouraging to the American people, but the American people are entitled to know the truth -- the bad news as well as the good news -- where the lives of our young men are involved.

Now let me turn, to a more encouraging report on another front.

At the time we launched our search for peace, I recognized we might not succeed in bringing an end to the war through negotiation.

I therefore put into effect another plan to bring peace -- a plan which will bring the war to an end regardless of what happens on the negotiating front. It is in line with a major shift in U.S. foreign policy which I described in my press conference at Guam on July 25.

Let me briefly explain what has been described as the Nixon doctrine -- a policy which will not only help end the war in Viet-Nam but which is an essential element of our program to prevent future Viet-Nams.

We Americans are a do-it-yourself people. We are an impatient people. Instead of teaching someone else to do a job, we like to do it ourselves. And this trait has been carried over into our foreign policy.

In Korea and again in Viet-Nam, the United States furnished most of the money, most of the arms, and most of the men to help the people of those countries defend their freedom against Communist aggression.

Before any American troops were committed to Viet-Nam,

a leader of another Asian country expressed this opinion to me when I was traveling in Asia as a private citizen. He said: "When you are trying to assist another nation defend its freedom, U.S. policy should be to help them fight the war, but not to fight the war for them."

Well, in accordance with this wise counsel, I laid down in Guam three principle as guidelines for future American policy toward Asia:

. First, the United States will keep all of its treaty commitments.

. Second, we shall provide a shield if a nuclear power threatens the freedom of a nation allied with us or of a nation whose survival we consider vital to our security.

. Third, in all cases involving other types of aggression, we shall furnish military and economic assistance when requested in accordance with our treaty commitments. But we shall look to the nation directly threatened to assume the primary responsibility of providing the manpower for its defense.

After I announced this policy, I found that the leaders of the Philippines, Thailand, Viet-Nam, South Korea, and other nations which might be threatened by Communist aggression welcomed this new direction in American foreign policy.

The defense of freedom is everybody's business -- not just America's business. And it is particularly the responsibility of the people whose freedom is threatened. In the previous administration we Americanized the war in Viet-Nam. In this administration we are Vietnamizing the search for peace.

The policy of the previous administration not only resulted in our assuming the primary responsibility for fighting the war but, even more significantly did not adequately stress the goal of strengthening the South Vietnamese so that they could defend themselves when we left.

The Vietnamization plan was launched following Secretary [of Defense Melvin] Laird's visit to Viet-Nam last March. Under the plan, I ordered first a substantial increase in the training and equipment of South Vietnamese forces.

In July, on my visit to Vietnam, I changed General Abrams' orders so that they were consistent with the objectives of our new policies. Under the new orders, the primary mission of

120

our troops is to enable the South Vietnamese forces to assume the full responsibility for the security of South Viet-Nam....

We have adopted a plan which we have worked out in cooperation with the South Vietnamese for the complete withdrawal of all U.S. combat ground forces and their replacement by South Vietnamese forces on an orderly timetable. This withdrawal will be made from strength and not from weakness. As South Vietnamese forces become stronger, the rate of American withdrawal can become greater....

If the level of infiltration or our casualties increase while we are trying to scale down fighting, it will be the result of a conscious decision by the enemy.

Hanoi could make no greater mistake than to assume that an increase in violence will be to its advantage. If I conclude that increased enemy action jeopardizes our remaining forces in Viet-Nam, I shall not hesitate to take strong and effective measures to deal with the situation.

This is not a threat. This is a statement of policy which as Commander in Chief of our Armed Forces I am making in meeting my responsibility for the protection of American fighting men wherever they may be.

My fellow Americans, I am sure you can recognize from what I have said that we really only have two choices open to us if we want to end this war:

. I can order an immediate, precipitate withdrawal of all Americans from Viet-Nam without regard to the effects of that action.

. Or we can persist in our search for a just peace, through negotiated settlement if possible or through continued implementation of our plan for Vietnamization if necessary-- a plan in which we will withdrawal all of our forces from Viet-Nam on a schedule in accordance with our program, as the South Vietnamese become strong enough to defend their own freedom.

I have chosen this second course. It is not the easy way. It is the right way. It is a plan which will end the war and serve the cause of peace, not just in Viet-Nam but in the Pacific and in the world.

In speaking of the consequences of a precipitate withdrawal,

121

I mentioned that our allies would lose confidence in America. Far more dangerous, we would lose confidence in ourselves. Oh, the immediate reaction would be a sense of relief that our men were coming home. But as we saw the consequences of what we had done, inevitable remorse and divisive recrimination would scar our spirit as a people....

I have chosen a plan for peace. I believe it will succeed.

Following this announcement, Nixon's popularity soared. It seemed that he really did have a plan for ending the war and achieving peace with honor. Though more than half of the American public in 1969 thought that the initial decision to enter the war was wrong, nearly 70% supported the Nixon Doctrine and Vietnamization. It appeared that things were beginning to go our way.

But the North Vietnamese chief negotiator at the Paris Peace Talks, Le Duc Tho, did not see things the same way. He saw America being torn in two over the issue of the war. He saw the U.S. Congress repeal the Gulf of Tonkin Resolution in 1970 thus limiting the president's power to pursue the war. He saw PAVN forces in Cambodia and Laos defeating the "new and improved" ARVN. He also saw the beginnings of U.S. withdrawal. The temporary nature of the U.S. presence in Vietnam once again became clear. He saw all these things and waited as had his ancestors who had fought and defeated the Chinese, the Japanese, and the French.

With new and improved Soviet weapons, the forces of the North decided to delay negotiations in Paris and press forward militarily in 1971 and 1972. Like the Americans, they too were hoping to negotiate from a position of strength. As American troop withdrawals accelerated and more of the war effort was placed on ARVN forces, the North began to see the light at the end of *its* tunnel. That light became clearer and clearer as more and more Americans left the stage.

By 1972, most American troops were being used in support positions and only about 6,000 in actual combat roles. Most of the war effort was then in the hands of the ARVN forces. Early in the year, combined forces of the PLAF and PAVN invaded South Vietnam from Cambodia and across the demilitarized zone that separated North and South Vietnam. They quickly swept away ARVN opposition in key northern and western provinces. It became clear that without renewed U.S. intervention, South Vietnam would quickly collapse.

President Nixon was faced with a difficult decision as to whether to restore U.S. ground forces and renew the fight or allow the collapse. Three constraints kept him from renewing American intervention. First, in February he had succeeded in splitting the communist monolith by establishing relations with Communist China. Also, the U.S. was moving closer to a policy of detente with the Soviets that would relax some of the tensions of the Cold War. Renewed intervention would put both of these policies in danger. Secondly, public opinion, it was clear, would support no renewed war effort that endangered the lives of U.S. troops. Thirdly, 1972 was an election year and he could not risk seeming more hawkish in light of public opinion and an increasingly dovish Democratic Party. However, something had to be done to prevent the collapse of the South before the November elections in the U.S. It was time for yet another fateful decision.

For the first time since 1969, Nixon announced the use of B-52's to bomb communist emplacements (fortified camps) in the South and in the North. The sweeping victories of the Communist forces in the South were stopped and Nixon attempted to further cut Communist supply lines by mining Haiphong harbor and attacking merchant ships anchored there. Laser guided "smart bombs" were first used in these attacks but the civilian toll in the North was enormous. Also enormous was the public outcry in Congress and on the streets in the U.S. To counter this, just prior to the November elections, Kissinger announced that a peace proposal was nearly complete and that "peace is at hand." Nixon was re-elected in a landslide.

Kissinger's announcement was premature. He knew full well that Thieu strongly objected to the peace plan but his announcement destroyed the one issue that the Democrats held over Nixon, his unrealized promise to end the war. Thieu's objections were conveniently not revealed. President Thieu was reluctant to sign an agreement that he felt would lead to his removal from office. To show support for Thieu, Nixon ordered the most devastating bombing raids of the war in December of 1972. Congress exploded with indignation and swore to cut off all funds for the war if a negotiated settlement was not quickly completed. A pledge of continued U.S. support for the Thieu regime and $2 billion in aid convinced the South Vietnamese to agree to a cease-fire.

The Paris Agreement, signed on January 27, 1973, declared a cease-fire in South Vietnam, froze forces of the North and the South in the positions they occupied, provided for the return of POW's, and created a joint council to work toward a lasting peace in Vietnam. Two months later, all U.S. forces had left Vietnam. For many Vietnamese, it seemed a re-enactment of the French withdrawal nearly two decades before. The question for many Americans was: did the U.S. leave with its honor and credibility intact or with a stigma that would take many years to erase?

After American Withdrawal

Though the U.S. withdrew its troops from South Vietnam in 1973, it left behind enormous supplies of munitions and a well-trained and immense (one million men) army. The communists realized that the struggle was not over. They continued to select carefully the time and place of battles leaving the ARVN forces always on the defensive. As the war of attrition dragged on, American supplies were quickly used up and the PAVN forces began to consistently beat the ARVN in set piece battles.

Domestically South Vietnam was in trouble too. The South Vietnamese economy began to suffer from enormous inflation and unemployment once the Americans left. Thieu became increasingly dictatorial, turning aside any semblance of democracy. He dismissed any cabinet or military official who challenged his decisions. Most importantly, Thieu refused to allow any of the political provisions of the Paris Agreement to come to fruition. He blocked any attempts at setting up nationwide elections, creating a coalition government, or in any way negotiating with the communists. The communist forces, in response to this, began in October of 1973 to plan a huge offensive against the South.

By the fall of 1974 Thieu was running out of men and munitions. Repeated defeats at the hands of the communists led to mass desertions from the ARVN. The U.S. Congress refused to resupply Thieu's army. The South Vietnamese economy was falling apart. PAVN forces began attacking major cities in South Vietnam. Whereas the cities had once been safe havens, they were now susceptible to communist attack. One after another, the major cities of South Vietnam fell. During a two week period in March of 1975, eight million South Vietnamese came under communist rule.

On April 21st of that year, Thieu resigned and was succeeded by General Minh who offered to negotiate with the communists. But it was too late. Nine days later, Saigon was totally in the control of the communists and all ARVN forces had laid down their weapons. The Second Indochina War was over and Vietnam was once again a single nation.

Chapter Twelve

Why We Lost, What We Learned

There can be no one reason that explains the failure of U.S. policy in Vietnam in the years 1955 to 1973. A close examination of those reasons allows us to group them into three categories; military, conceptual, and political. We could also categorize these factors as internal to the U.S., internal to Vietnam, and external or international constraints. In this chapter we will review these factors and explore explanations of some of the lessons the U.S. learned from the Vietnam experience.

Fighting the War

Many military historians today argue that the reason the war was lost was insufficient or improperly used firepower. Many factors help explain this argument. American soldiers had difficulty adapting to the hot, wet climate and often fell victim to malaria. The North Vietnamese soldiers were well schooled in guerilla warfare and used their skill successfully against an American army better trained to fight in open battle. These techniques of guerilla warfare also took a mental toll on American soldiers. Booby traps were particularly brutal and were often designed to maim, not kill. The Vietnamese also held the initiative in the field of battle as *they* decided when they would fight. Another factor was the way each soldier looked at time. The North Vietnamese were resigned to a protracted war; the Americans wanted to get it over with as quickly as possible.

It was also very difficult to measure who was winning at any given time. Ground gained meant little and body counts became the only means of assessing victory or defeat. Another problem lay in the policy of gradual escalation. The slow but steady increase in American forces gave the enemy time to adapt and reinforce. By the time U.S. forces reached their peak, support for the war back at home was beginning to dwindle.

But perhaps the most compelling reason for the U.S. defeat, from the military standpoint, was the fact that the U.S. military consistently underestimated the will, the power, and the effectiveness of the Communist forces. American arrogance led us to believe that the communist forces would quickly surrender to such a vastly superior, armed adversary. This was a mistake that would not be repeated in Grenada, Panama, or Kuwait.

Faulty Assumptions

American policy makers based their decisions on assumptions that were dated and questionable. The U.S. believed that communism was monolithic and every communist state took its directions from Moscow or Peking. In truth, North Vietnam hated and feared the

Chinese and paid little attention to Moscow. American policy was also based on the Domino Theory. This idea, though popularly accepted, was never really tested on the world stage. Also, it was not applicable in Vietnam since this was not a war of communist expansionism but a civil war designed to reunite two halves of the same country.

The Culture Gap

The U.S. has always been a very ethnocentric culture, that is, we hold an attitude that our nation and its ideals are superior to the ideals and cultures of others. Americans assumed that the people of South Vietnam would welcome the chance to become a democratic nation. They failed to realize that questions of daily survival were more important to the Vietnamese than political ideology. Americans also failed to realize the importance of Buddhism. Destroying ancestral graveyards and temples through bombing alienated much of the population as did the policy of favoring Catholics over Buddhists in government positions. One of the great ironies of the war was the fact that the U.S. ended up destroying a country it was trying to save. Also, the U.S. failed to find a leader in the South who could capture the imagination of the peasants *and* follow through on the policies the U.S. wanted. The South became totally dependent on the U.S., militarily, politically, and economically. That was hardly the way to build a new and independent nation.

Domestic Dissent

It is very difficult to assess the impact of the anti-war movement. Some argue that it gave aid to the enemy by demonstrating a lack of unity in the U.S. Others say that it hurt the cause of peace once it became identified with the counterculture of sex, drugs, and rock and roll. Violent demonstrations also alienated people. Though the most violent demonstrations caught the public eye, the movement was diverse and largely peaceful. Songwriters like Bob Dylan, Arlo Guthrie, and Phil Ochs pointed out the hypocrisy of American foreign policy. Theaters produced *Hair*, a play about the counterculture. Peaceful demonstrations emphasized themes of love, compassion, and togetherness. Still, the movement appears to have had little direct effect on policy makers. Presidents Nixon and Johnson largely ignored demonstrations and instead relied on opinion polls to indicate the mood of the public. And though support for the war declined, support for Presidential policy remained high throughout the war.

But the movement did serve to educate Americans and call attention to the nature of the conflict. Anti-war demonstrators did what the government would not: challenge the basic assumptions that guided the war effort. Years later, the debate over whether these people were heroes or traitors rages on. This is one question of the war that will probably never be settled.

The Lessons Learned: The U.S. in the Persian Gulf

Historians have called Vietnam "the unwinnable war" and the Persian Gulf War of 1991 "the Nintendo war." These two expressions oversimplify both conflicts but they also say a lot about the nature of each. Questions have arisen about comparing the two wars. What was so different in the execution of these two wars? Why did one go on for many years with no success and why was the other one completed successfully in such a short time?

What lessons were learned in Vietnam and applied in the Persian Gulf? To answer these questions, we must first look at some of the fundamental differences between the two wars.

First, Iraq, unlike North Vietnam, was totally isolated from its major suppliers. World opinion condemned the actions of Iraq and the Allies successfully blockaded and prevented the resupply of Iraq. Though the Soviets and the Chinese took no active role in the fighting, they were supportive of the UN resolutions. Thus, unlike the Vietnam War, fears of Soviet or Chinese intervention could be eliminated. Second, Allied forces did not have to deal with the jungle terrain of Southeast Asia in fighting the war in Kuwait and Iraq. The nature of this war was more in line with the type of war that the U.S. is best equipped to fight: the set-piece war that relies heavily on planes and artillery. The vast technological advantages the U.S. enjoyed were more significant in the Gulf War. New technology overwhelmed the Iraqis and limited civilian casualties. Third, victory in the Gulf was easily measurable in terms of ground gained and targets destroyed. Also important was the incorporation of the Middle Eastern Allies. There was no battle for the hearts and minds of the Kuwaitis. These were key differences in the two wars. But what lessons of Vietnam were applied in the Persian Gulf?

Military leaders often cite the reason for the loss of Vietnam as being that they were limited by political considerations. They blame politicians for not allowing them to go ahead and win the war with a massive effort. President Bush gave his military commanders great control over the war in the Gulf. He wanted a quick and decisive

131

victory through massive firepower. He pledged early on that the war in the Gulf would not be "another Vietnam."

Another lesson of Vietnam that was applied in the Gulf was the handling of the press. Some argue that the press presented a very one-sided view of the war in Vietnam and thereby hurt the war effort by turning public opinion against the war. The press was strictly limited in what it could report in the Gulf. Some argue that this censorship was necessary to protect the lives of service men and women stationed there. Others say that the military was trying to avoid any negative reports that might decrease the widespread support for the war in the U.S. These critics argue that the military went too far in limiting the press. There is no disputing the fact that the press did not enjoy the same freedom in reporting in the Gulf as it did in Vietnam.

Probably the biggest lesson learned was a twofold military lesson; don't underestimate your enemy and don't gradually escalate the war. Both of these lessons were applied in the Gulf. The Allies waited and patiently built their ground forces to the point where they enjoyed parity with the Iraqi forces. All the while they were waiting, bombs and artillery were destroying the war-making ability of Iraq. The Persian Gulf War was a massive, decisive strike at the Iraqis. The gradual escalation of the war in Vietnam gave time for communist forces to adapt and fortify themselves against the growing U.S. forces. The other important military decision was to over-, not under-, estimate the power of Saddam Hussein. By doing so, the U.S. military was prepared for any eventuality from chemical to biological or even nuclear war. Over estimating the enemy prevents any embarrassing surprises

132

and helps bring about swift success.

The analysis above relates some but not all of the legacy of Vietnam. Historians will debate and compare the Vietnam and Persian Gulf Wars for years to come. Look back over the previous readings and try to answer the following questions.

Checkpoint

1. When military leaders argue that the politicians lost the Vietnam War, what political realities are they ignoring?

2. In your opinion, could the Vietnam War have been won as quickly and decisively as the war in the Gulf? Why or why not?

3. What was different about the makeup of the U.S. Armed Forces in these two wars? Did that have any effect on the outcome?

4. From a public policy standpoint, what factors shaped U.S. policy in the Gulf? How were those factors different in the two wars?

Chapter Thirteen

The Costs of the War

In her award-winning book, *In Country*, author Bobby Ann Mason describes the lives of several Vietnam Veterans in the early 1980's. The social and personal costs of Vietnam can be derived from this fictional account; guilt, nightmares, cancer, birth defects, unemployment, drug abuse, and a host of other disorders affect these Veterans. Some become so distraught with the memory of the war that they even sometimes envy their buddies who didn't make it back. Some work for a healing of the wounds of the war through support groups. Others cannot accept help, they can only accept guilt and remorse for having their lives, and those of the Vietnamese, changed forever by the war. The costs of the Vietnam War are difficult to quantify and that has made it difficult for policy makers to deal effectively with these costs. How do we place a dollar sign on lost innocence, nightmares, and stress disorders? How do we now use public policy to salve these wounds? What responsibilities are we willing to admit and what costs are we willing to pay? These are the challenges that remain.

Some costs are easy to quantify but difficult to grasp the meaning of. More than 58,000 Americans died in combat-related incidents in Vietnam. More than 40,000 others died in non-combat situations in and around Vietnam. It is estimated that more than 50,000 Vietnam Veterans have taken their own lives since returning. The 58,000 names on the Vietnam War Memorial in Washington, D.C. tell only part of the story. The rest of the story is much more difficult to put into numbers.

For Vets and families of those listed as missing in action (MIA), the uncertainty of their loved ones' fate is a daily torment. About 1700 servicemen are still listed as MIA. About half that number are classified as Killed in Action but their remains were never recovered. The fate of the remaining MIA's has been the center of much speculation. Veteran's groups feel that the North Vietnamese have not done everything they could and should to account for those still listed as missing. Some groups feel that Vietnam still holds American prisoners of war (POW's). Movies like *Rambo* helped popularize these ideas. Vietnam maintains that all American servicemen and their remains have been sent back to the U.S. This is probably the case. Vietnam has nothing to gain by holding back. But for thousands of fellow soldiers and family members who did not have the chance to bury their dead, the issue is very much alive. Years later, parents, wives, and children continue to expect the front door to open and for their loved ones to return.

Another unresolved issue is that of Agent Orange poisoning of American G.I.'s. Agent Orange was a powerful chemical defoliant used to destroy the jungle canopy that provided cover to the communist forces. It contained dioxin, one of the most powerful and deadly poisons known to humankind. Over five million acres of South Vietnam were laid waste by the application of Agent Orange. The chemicals were released into the air when foliage burned and leached into the water supply. American soldiers inhaled the smoke and drank and bathed in the water. Today, many of these soldiers suffer from a serious skin disease called chloracne. Veterans exposed to Agent Orange show abnormally high rates of cancer and have an unusually high rate of birth defects among their children. Others suffer from severe headaches. The Veterans Administration (VA), is charged with providing medical care to Veterans who suffer from service-related illnesses. Until quite recently, the VA has been reluctant to provide help to Veterans suffering from Agent Orange poisoning. The VA claims that there was no hard evidence linking these disorders and Agent Orange. Today Veterans can be treated for these problems if they can prove they were exposed to Agent Orange. The issue of compensation for widows, and for children with birth defects, remains unresolved.

One of the most difficult issues to deal with is PTSD, post-traumatic stress disorder. This is a delayed reaction experienced by Vets after they return home. It manifests itself in many ways ranging from headaches to violent behavior to drug abuse and even suicide. Many of the homeless on America's streets are Vets suffering from PTSD. In previous wars it may have been called shell shock or combat fatigue. But the rate of these disorders for Vietnam Vets is twice that of any previous war. Many factors contribute to this alarming statistic. Veterans returned to a country that was neither proud nor grateful for their service in Vietnam. Many were fighting a war that they felt had no meaning. Many deserted; over

600,000 soldiers received less than honorable discharges. The average age of the soldier in Vietnam was 19; in WWII, 26. The rotation of personnel made it difficult to form lasting relationships. Soldiers new to the fighting were considered prime targets for the communist forces. This contributed to feelings of loneliness and isolation. The nature of guerilla warfare was a constant stress on the nerves of the soldier as was the hot, wet weather. Many felt guilty over the tactics of search and destroy and could not deal with a war that was measured in body counts and kill ratios. All of these factors contribute to PTSD. But because of the erratic nature of the symptoms of PTSD, it is difficult for the Vietnam vet to receive needed attention. Sometimes Vets choose to refuse help. Those who do may use the pain of PTSD to help deal with the guilt they feel over their role in Vietnam.

Attempts to Help the Vietnam Vet

It is one of the great tragedies of American history that we have been so slow to deal with the pain of the Vietnam Vet. The Veterans Administration, faced with cutbacks in funding after the war, has been reluctant to acknowledge the special needs of the Vietnam Vet. Treatment for Agent Orange victims and sufferers from PTSD would be extremely costly. Veterans groups have kept up the pressure on policy-makers and today more services are available. President Bush created a Cabinet level position to deal with Veterans' affairs. But it should also be noted that official recognition of the Vietnam Vet is still withheld. Vietnam Veterans were not welcomed home with ticker tape parades as was the custom for Veterans of WWII. Very few policy makers have expressed gratitude for the sacrifices of these soldiers. That responsibility has been shouldered by Veterans' groups. The Vietnam War Memorial, the dedication ceremony for that memorial, and the subsequent reading of all 58,000 names at the Washington Cathedral were all organized and paid for by Veterans' groups. Neither the President, the Vice-President, nor any Cabinet member attended the ceremony at the Cathedral. Nothing reinforces the guilt and the pain of Vietnam Vets like the withholding of recognition from the government they served.

Economic Costs

President Johnson, from 1965 to 1968 was trying to fight two wars at once, the war in Vietnam and the War on Poverty at home. Both were incredibly expensive but he resisted the need to raise taxes for fear of losing public support for his agenda. The costs of these wars and the resulting deficit financing led to high interest rates, inflation, and unemployment. This disruption of the economy continued through 1982. Trade-offs had to be made in trying to fulfill the dual agenda and many Great Society programs just ran out of money. LBJ's dream of eliminating poverty in America was destroyed by the expenses of the war. Today's estimates on the cost of the Vietnam war are in excess of one trillion dollars.

Political Costs

Of more interest to policy makers are the political costs of the war. The lies that were exposed in the investigation of the Gulf of Tonkin incident shook the American public's confidence in the government. *The New York Times* exposed the political and military ineptitude of U.S. policy in the war by the publishing of the *Pentagon Papers*.

Richard Nixon bombed Cambodia despite pre-election promises to avoid widening the war. He then fell victim to his own paranoia over secrecy and resigned his office in the wake of the Watergate scandal. The war cost LBJ his presidency and the Democratic Party the elections of 1968 and 1972. Jimmy Carter seemed to be paralyzed by the actions of Iran and his critics called this reluctance to get involved militarily overseas the "Vietnam Syndrome."

All of these factors have contributed to a general sense of apathy among the American public. We distrust government and many express this by refusing to vote. We have lost faith in our elected leaders. The word politician carries the same negative connotations as it did in the Gilded Age, the worst era of political bankruptcy in American history. Today's American sees government as wasteful, detached, corrupt, and deceitful. Voter participation is alarmingly low. We are disillusioned with our leaders and too complacent to do anything about it. This may prove to be the most devastating cost of the war. The country that has become synonymous with democracy doesn't seem to care enough to exercise its democratic responsibilities anymore.

There is also an important lesson to be learned about the formation of public policy by the executive branch. The Vietnam War is a case study in the use and abuse of presidential power. As the war progressed, the circle of men making decisions, important public policy decisions, grew smaller and smaller. Debate was confined within the administration. The war-making power of Congress was ignored. The carefully crafted system of checks and balances was corrupted. Congress grew complacent and the imperial presidency, a broadening of the powers of the executive, grew. Laws were broken with impunity. As the Congress and the Courts slept, the White House expanded its power and prestige. Power was concentrated in the hands of an elite few.

With such a legacy, it is no wonder that George Bush disputed the need for Congressional approval for his actions in the Persian Gulf War. But Congress in 1991 was more assertive and reminded the American public that Congress, and only Congress, has the power to make war. President Bush relented to this call from Congress, then sought and received from Congress approval for military actions in the Gulf. (However, it should be noted that the military buildup prior to the offensive was done without Congressional approval - an example of the continuing power of the imperial presidency.)

So we see that the costs of the war occur on many levels, personal, economic, and political. The challenge for policymakers today is to realize these costs and deal with them. We must strive to keep the decision-making process open to public debate whenever and wherever possible. Too narrow a concentration of the power, to make and implement public policy threatens our democracy. The Framers of the Constitution kept this in mind throughout the Convention. It is a lesson we cannot afford to forget.

Checkpoint

Discuss each of the following questions. Develop policies to deal with each situation. Keep in mind the economic constraints we face today. Try to answer in each case what you would do and how you would pay for it.

1. Why has the federal government been reluctant to recognize the Vietnam Vet? Is it too late for us to do anything today as a nation to correct this? What would you recommend? How does the recognition given to the soldiers returning from the Persian Gulf affect this?

2. What can be done to get the American public back into the voting booths? How can we encourage policy makers to be honest and help them regain the trust of the American public?

3. What could be done to finally resolve the issue of POW's and MIA's still unaccounted for in Vietnam? What role has the media, TV and the movies, played in this situation?

4. If a definite causal link is established between Agent Orange and cancer and birth defects, who, if anyone, should reimburse the victims? the U.S. government? the makers of Agent Orange? Should reimbursement be made to sufferers of PTSD? How would you determine amounts in each case? Who would pay?

5. Let us assume that a link is established between Agent Orange and severe health disorders. Should we compensate victims in Vietnam? Why or why not?

Chapter Fourteen

The Final Question - Vietnam Today

One final question remains for which we and our policymakers must forge an answer: what is to be our relationship with Vietnam in the 1990's? It is important for us to look at the issues that divide our two countries and to ask if those wounds, still open and bleeding, can and should be healed.

Vietnam is today a communist nation. It is a virtual police state maintaining one of the largest standing armies in the world. It has been involved in a war with its neighbor Kampuchea (formerly Cambodia). Vietnam is rigidly controlled by the military. It is also desperately poor.

The U.S. occupation forces propped up the economy of the South with American aid and the spending American soldiers did while stationed there during the war. Once the Americans left, the South Vietnamese economy collapsed. The North was also in bad shape financially. Much of its limited industrial base and infrastructure

143

(roads, bridges, services) were destroyed in the bombing. Massive population shifts occurred in the South as peasants moved from the countryside to the comparative safety of the cities. Overcrowding, prostitution, drug abuse, unemployment, and malnutrition became epidemic in the cities. Once united, Vietnam turned to the world community for economic aid to help rebuild. The U.S. placed severe trade embargoes on Vietnam and helped defeat attempts by the Vietnamese to secure loans through the International Monetary Fund, an international bank designed to help developing countries by providing low cost loans. The Vietnamese turned to the Soviets for aid but found most of that aid in the form of low cost loans to buy Soviet-made weapons.

Slowly, Vietnam has once again become self-sufficient agriculturally. But it is still desperate for a source of foreign capital needed to purchase machinery and fuel to begin industrialization. With the Soviets in deep economic trouble, Vietnam has approached the U.S. about relaxing trade barriers and even opening a naval base on Vietnam's coast. The question for American policy-makers then becomes, under what conditions, if any, do we re-establish relations with Vietnam? What issues need to be resolved in order for this rapprochement (the process of reestablishing friendly relations) process to begin?

The most emotional issue still attached to the war for Americans is the MIA/POW issue. Vietnam would need to open its records and its borders to Americans who wished to search for clues as to the death or whereabouts of loved ones. Even so, many Americans would continue to resist rapprochement. Years of distrust and hate are not easily forgotten.

The most important issue from the standpoint of the U.S. government is Vietnam's role in Southeast Asia. Vietnam's huge army has invaded and occupied parts of neighboring Kampuchea. The U.S. has said that Vietnam must renounce expansionism and help create a stable Southeast Asia before any economic or political ties are re-established. As an incentive to this, the U.S. has relaxed restrictions on exporting medical supplies to Vietnam and many private organizations in the U.S. have attempted to help the country with humanitarian aid. Formal recognition will only come when Vietnam de-militarizes its society and works toward a lasting peace in the region. As of the spring of 1991, Vietnam has begun to move in this direction and has removed most of its forces from Kampuchea.

For some Americans other issues also need to be addressed. These issues spring directly from the conduct of the war and the soldiers fighting it. American servicemen acquitted themselves with courage and compassion but they also left behind a terrible birthright, thousands of Amerasian children who are looked on as the lowest class in Vietnamese society. Some Vets have attempted to adopt Amerasian orphans or provide support for families in Vietnam. Some Vietnamese families have successfully immigrated to the U.S.

The saddest casualties of any war are the children. Children in Vietnam during the war, now as adults, suffer from cancer and birth defects caused by Agent Orange. Thousands of others lost limbs and suffer today from the terrible lack of wheelchairs and prosthetic devices (artificial limbs). Many Vets and other Americans feel compassion for the suffering of these Vietnamese and they support organizations that try to reduce the pain of the Vietnamese people. Others have become active in the movement to reconcile the peoples of Vietnam and the U.S. These people have successfully put the war behind them and they are actively trying to heal the wounds of the war both in the U.S. and in Vietnam. The U.S. became allied with Japan and Germany in the aftermath of WWII; perhaps the same reconciliation will occur with the Vietnamese.

Checkpoint

1. Find out what organizations in your community are concerned with this issue. Veterans organizations? Helping Hands organizations? What is their stand? What are they doing?

2. How were Japan and Germany treated by the U.S. in the aftermath of WWII? Why was Vietnam treated so differently?

3. Write a letter to your U.S. Senator or Representative expressing your feelings on reconciliation with Vietnam. Limit your letter to 200 to 400 words. Be concise and clear in your arguments.

Bibliography

DeBenedetti, Charles. *An American Ordeal: The Antiwar Movement of the Vietnam Era.* Syracuse, NY: Syracuse University Press, 1990.

Duiker, William J. "Introduction to Vietnam: Land, History, and Culture" in *The Lessons of the Vietnam War.* The Center for Social Studies Education, 1988.

Goodwin, Jim, Psy.D. "Readjustment Problems Among Vietnam Veterans", Cincinnati: Disabled American Veterans.

Herring, George C. "America and Vietnam: The Debate Continues".

Herring, George C. "Why the United States Failed in Vietnam" from "The Vietnam Syndrome and American Foreign Policy", The Virginia Quarterly Review, LVII, Fall, 1981.

Kahin, George McT. *Intervention: How America Became Involved in Vietnam.* Garden City, NY: Anchor Books, 1987.

Kattenburg, Paul M. *The Vietnam Trauma in American Foreign Policy, 1945-75.* New Brunswick, NJ: Transaction Books, 1980.

Kimball, Jeffrey P. *To Reason Why: The Debate About the Causes of U.S. Involvement in the Vietnam War.* New

York: McGraw-Hill, 1990.

McMahon, Robert J. ed. *Major Problems in the History of the Vietnam War.* Lexington, MA: D.C. Heath, 1990.

Small, Melvin. *Johnson, Nixon, and the Doves.* New Brunswick, NJ: Rutgers University Press, 1988.

Turley, William S. *The Second Indochina War: A Short Political and Military History, 1954-1975.* New York: New American Library, 1986.

Wilcox, Fred. "The Wounds of War and the Process of Healing" in *The Lessons of the Virtnam War.* The Center for Social Studies Education, 1988.

Woodside, Alexander. "Vietnamese History: Confucianism, Colonialism, and the Struggle for Independence".

Young, Marilyn B. *The Vietnam Wars 1945-1990.* New York: HarperCollins, 1991.